NAVIG[
RESISTING PUB[

DAEJAH L. MERRILL

Copyright © Daejah Merrill. All rights reserved. No part of this book may be reproduced or used in any manner without the prior written permission of the copyright owner, except for the use of brief quotations in a book review.

All scriptures quotations marked NKJV are taken from the Holy Bible, New King James Version. All scriptures quotations marked KJV are taken from the Holy Bible, King James Version. All scriptures quotations marked NLT are taken from the Holy Bible, New Living Translation. All scriptures quotations marked AMPC are taken from the Holy Bible, Amplified Bible, Classic Edition .All scriptures quotations marked NIV are taken from the Holy Bible, New International Version. All scriptures quotations marked TPT are taken from the Holy Bible, The Passion Translation.

Paperback : 978-1-7351153-3-7

Cover design by Asha Morris
Layout by Daejah Merrill

I dedicate this book to my Apostle Jonathan McGee and the founder of 13:46 Dance Ensemble, Jeanna Booker. Thank you for being my blueprint, calling forth, and cultivating me into who God said I am. When I, the student, was ready both of my teachers appeared. You have both played vital roles in my development and have pushed me to discover and own who God has created me to be. Thank you for saying yes to God and obeying the call to lead, mentor, and cultivate people like me, may nothing that you have poured out ever be wasted.

CONTENTS

Acknowledgements III

Foreward by Jonathan McGee VII

Becoming an Active Participant XI

Part 1: What is Obscurity?

CHAPTER 1: Obscurity Defined 1

CHAPTER 2: My Journey 11

CHAPTER 3: Signs of Obscurity 17

CHAPTER 4: Responding To the Call 27

Part 2: Purpose of Obscurity

CHAPTER 5: The Power of Obscurity 37

CHAPTER 6: Living A Life Worthy of the Calling 43

CHAPTER 7: Components of Identity 53

CHAPTER 8: Prophetic Processing 59

Part 3: Navigating Obscurity

CHAPTER 9: Enemies of Obscurity 85

CHAPTER 10: Friends of Obscurity 97

CHAPTER 11: From Coping To Conquering 105

CHAPTER 12: Responding to God's Invitation 109

v

FOREWORD

The Scripture is clear: "except a grain fall to the ground and die it abides alone". The process of becoming fruitful in your life, calling, and purpose requires us all to go through a season of being buried alive. I could tell you countless stories of the devastation that comes before elevation. Often, I thought, am I being picked on? Why is this happening to me? The truth was that the chosen don't really get a choice. The faster we learn that our destiny is wiser than us, the quicker we're able to navigate the deepest disappointments that comes with the process.

God has mighty plans for all of us; those plans have been preordained for us to walk in, and those plans don't come without navigating pain. Pain has a way of proving who we are to ourselves. Wait! Yes, I was very clear. Your destiny will vet your soul and prove that you're made up of champion blood. No more proving to others who we are when we haven't discovered it ourselves. Owning your identity is to be okay with the process of becoming; understanding destiny isn't just an arrival but who you become.

God has a protocol for your life and purpose. Often, God uses "wilderness seasons" to produce mighty ones. Remember, young David was sent to work with sheep when he was called as a king. Think of Moses, who spent 40 years in the wilderness developing his leadership ability. Consider young Joesph, who spent years in a prison only to become the leading economic leader in his time. You see, obscurity isn't a death sentence; it's a developing one. It's like being in a dark room until the photo is processed. God makes all things beautiful in His time. Your Time is Now.

In her newest book, "Navigating Obscurity," Daejah Merrill takes you on a life-transforming journey. Replete with knowledge and principles that empower the reader to stay the course of becoming while conquering obscurity. Resisting being seen to be properly developed. This book is both powerful and empowering. With every chapter, the writer brings you along on her journey of development, sharing transparent and vulnerable moments and providing wisdom and insight gained along the way. It's my pleasure to write this forward for my Spiritual Daughter. Having a front-row seat in her journey and obedience to the father, I encourage you to take to heart the pages and practice the principles. Your life will never be the same.

- Jonathan McGee
Founder of Jonathan McGee International

BECOMING AN ACTIVE PARTICIPANT

If you picked this book up, I am pretty sure you have already received salvation and have found yourself in the middle of who God says you are and your current reality. What God said you'll do and what you have done. You have so much to look forward to because you have God's word, but you are having a hard time navigating how to get from where you are now to where he said you will be. You have replayed the prophecy recordings and reread your journals full of visions and dreams that God has shown you, yet you find yourself in the middle of what he said and the word being made a reality in your life. Congratulations, you have made it to your season of obscurity; welcome to your personal journey of developing for and in God!

At times, this journey may seem lonely, dark, and meaningless, but in fact, it is one of the most vital seasons for longevity in God. You are not here by coincidence in fact, you are right on schedule in the plan of God. I know that truth just freed so many people because sometimes we are so focused on our intended destination that we miss the present and valuable moments in the process. You must develop trust in God and patience with his sovereign will over your life and know that God doesn't waste any time or season of life; in fact, your life has been planned out (Psalm 139:16) from the very beginning of time and by the grace of God we have not been left to navigate life alone but he gave us everything we need in order to live a godly life (2 Peter 1:3-4). God gave us his Holy Spirit to lead and guide us through the prosperous life he has intended for us to live.

Allow me to take you on a journey of understanding what obscurity is, the purpose of it, and how to navigate through it with wisdom, joy, and hope in your final out-come. Once you understand through the lens of God the why and how concerning any season of life, you will learn what you need to do in order to become an active partici-pant instead of a resistant bystander. No season is wasted; every season brings glory to God, even if you seem hidden.

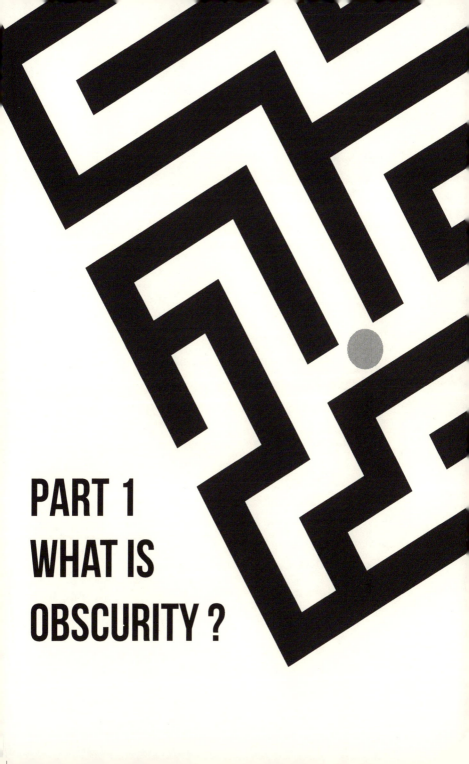

PART 1
WHAT IS
OBSCURITY ?

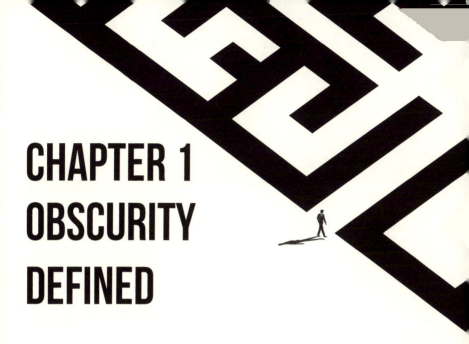

CHAPTER 1
OBSCURITY DEFINED

The place of obscurity is when you are hidden in plain sight. It feels like nobody sees you, knows you, or understands you, resulting in you feeling misunderstood, unknown, and rejected, which can be an emotional trigger for many that may have encountered these emotions in the past. You must first understand that it may be the same emotions arising but a different situation and/or purpose, which means it is not intended to be processed the same way. You must first allow this place of pain caused by rejection in your past to be healed so you can fully embrace this intended place of process for the will of God in your life.

Obscurity is experienced on both ends; the viewer and the person themselves are unaware of who they are and who they have yet to become. This is an internally conflicting place to be, especially with no understanding of its intentions. Obscurity can be hard for those who struggle with insecurity, pride, and rejection. When you are insecure, you feel the need to be in the spotlight, and you crave attention to feel good about your self worth. When you are rejected, you are always looking to be received and/or affirmed by man. You always feel the need to be defended and always be right. When you have pride, you fall into the trap of comparison because you are not able to exalt others above yourself and be meek and humble when you are not in the forefront.

Obscurity is hard for those who have an unhealthy desire to be used by God because your works determine your worth. It's hard for those who value their accomplishments and works for God more than knowing God and value perfecting their gift over sharpening character and learning to live a life that can house your calling.

I know these things because it was very challenging for me, but I thank God that the season of obscurity exposed it, because none of these qualities are useful in fulfilling the call of God on your life. This season starts with exposure but should end with you conquering all that was revealed in your soul. With great discernment and understanding of how God develops prophetic people, I

> *"This season starts with exposure but should end with you conquering all that was revealed in your soul"*

have learned to process God's processing differently and see the fruits of growth it bears. I have learned how to submit to this season and gain wisdom on the way. I have realized how the enemy tries to get us to skip this part, and this part is so important because when you submit to obscurity, you find value in knowing God and private devotion and development instead of public praise or acknowledgment. Seasons of obscurity is God calling you to himself for you to grasp who he is, who you are, and get language for who he has called you to be, where he is sending you, and his intentions for you. This season requires great focus, consecration, and intentional time with God. You have to learn fellowship with the Holy Spirit, because he is your empowering agent, leader into all truth, and the gateway to living and flowing in the supernatural. The Holy Spirit is God's gift to us, and it allows us to live our life here on earth as spirit beings unto God. I have learned that developing a relationship with the Holy Spirit takes seeking, worshiping, praying in the spirit, and, most importantly, waiting with expectation as you commune with God spirit to spirit.

I remember there were seasons where all I prayed about was my problems. It really taught me how to pray, but then, there came a time when it seemed like life was fine and settling down, and I was content, so I would come to my prayer time with no requests or petitions and I found myself not knowing what to say or do, and so I started forsaking my secret place because I had all I needed, I didn't learn God as a vital necessity. Yet, he was just my savior when needed but was not yet my friend that I valued fellowshipping with always. He was the one I ran to for defense, not realizing that he designed me to be on the offense, always in the know and gaining strategies to reign through life victoriously. When life got content, and I was no longer warring for deliverance or breakthrough in a certain area, in this awkward and sometimes uncomfortable stillness, I just kept hearing, "fellowship with me, spend time with me in my presence, and become one with me. ABIDE HERE."

This was an invitation into deeper levels of fellowship and greater realms of glory with God that I was not willing to miss. This invitation for more deserved a response; even if I was unsure of the destination, I realized God was calling me in closer to him to reveal me to me and reveal his plans and intentions for my life at a greater level. I would no longer just hear who I was based off of what people saw and discerned, but I would come to know it for myself because of divine encounters, visitations, and revelations that could only be accessed through a greater level of intimacy with God, which comes by building a prayer life.

All throughout the Bible, we see God calling ordinary people to do magnificent things that can only be done through his power, wisdom, and strength. God called people to himself and gave them an assignment that they were aware of and were able to boldly declare and operate with confidence and assurance because not only did they have an understanding of their purpose and calling, but they knew God was with them because they knew Him and spent time with him. We must understand and believe this truth. God has great plans of prosperity for you, and he desires for you to know them; this revelation is not hidden from you but for you. This revelation of who you are is meant to be

OBSCURITY DEFINED

sought out, investigated, developed, and tried, which may take some time, which is why the season of obscurity exists.

> *Jeremiah 29: 11 (AMPC)*
> *11 For I know the thoughts and plans that I have for you, says the Lord, thoughts, and plans for welfare and peace and not for evil, to give you hope in your final outcome.*

The burden of this book is seeing the lack of development of prophetic people, which leads to an unfulfilled purpose of God. The purpose of this book is to help people who are going through prophetic processing to help bring an understanding of the mindset and heart posture one needs in order to go through the process properly and give them hope for all that will be gained through it all, I desire to help you see the beauty of your hidden seasons, so you won't give into the temptation to skip it chasing opportunities to be seen, used, and affirmed without the proper lifestyle, intentions, and instructions to carry it out to completion.

Most times, the reason you are frustrated with a season is because you have not discerned the times, so you could be trying to harvest in a season where God is saying plant; because you have not discerned the times, you are ignorant of the required instructions and wisdom in order to partner with God for his promised results. So we must remember there is a time and a season for everything, and if you do not discern properly, you will be in a cycle of disappointment and frustration which leads to disbelief and bitterness with God, which leads to spiritual death because you have no faith in God. So, there is such a thing as doing all the right things at the wrong time, and you receive no results.

When you are out of alignment, life is going on, but you are not a participant with God; you have become his enemy, continuously resisting him and fighting against him with your actions and your unrenewed mind, so you then become an enemy to your life and God because you are ignorant of his intentions and his ways so instead of partnering with him you are fighting against him unknowingly. When we get God's will for our life, we must agree with his will and submit to His way of getting there. Most times, when we receive an exciting word from God, we try to make it happen on our own, and we must realize that if we want his will, we have to do it his way, and all he needs from us is our faith and our willing and submitted participation in the process.

"The purpose of obscurity is to become one with your divine self, which is the part of you that looks like Christ, your spirit"

The purpose of obscurity is to become one with your divine self, which is the part of you that looks like Christ, your spirit. It is the process or journey of coming into agreement and becoming one with Him, gaining knowledge of who you are and your assignment, and organizing your life to operate as that so you live a lifestyle that is worthy of your calling. Obscurity is the place of conquering all that resists and hinders your calling and helps you develop the things that matter to the effectiveness and longevity of your ministry.

OBSCURITY DEFINED

> *Psalm 139:14 (TPT)*
> *14 I thank you, God, for making me so mysteriously complex! Everything you do is marvelously breathtaking. It simply amazes me to think about it! How thoroughly you know me, Lord!*

We first have to understand that God has made us to be complex beings, and he is the only one who thoroughly knows us. In order to become self-aware we must go to our creator to understand who we are. This work will take some digging. We must allow God to reveal his original intent for our lives and how he created us to be in this world. You have to go through the process of healing and renewing your mind to the truth that I am not my past, I am not what happened to me, I am not my trauma, and I do not have to remain in bondage to the narratives the experience that I have encountered in my life has created for me. You first have to allow God to rewrite your story and allow him to reveal all he knows about you and who he originated from the beginning before you were born and sent into this earth so you can operate and live from this place. Our real life is hidden in him. This brings me to the first truth that all believers must understand, " we are spirit first." This is a truth that changed my mindset, changed the way that I viewed myself, my relationship with God, and how I navigate life.

I didn't approach life as a spiritual being first, but as one who lived in a body and possessed a soul. It made me realize that I was spending too much time in the natural realms and not enough in the spiritual realms that are available and legally accessible to me through the blood of Jesus. When you understand that you are spirit first, when you wake up in the morning, the first thing you should engage with is God in the spirit. When we engage with God, he sees us as a spirt. When we worship God, he tells us to worship in spirit and truth, not flesh, so in order to engage with God, you come to him as a spirit, meaning void of carnality and truth, which requires vulnerability. When I first got saved, I was not given this understanding that I am spiritual first and that from this place is how I rule and reign in the earth and have dominion and live victoriously. Your real victory in life only comes from living a life in unity with Christ.

Because we are complex beings, you must embrace the journey of discovering who God has called you to be and what he has called you to do. This journey happens when you are hidden and obscure. This moment isn't when you first receive salvation, embrace the love of God, and begin your journey of becoming a new creature in Christ. This season of obscurity begins when you come to the awareness that there is a call from God on your life, and you have made a conscious decision to respond to it by investigating and growing and developing into that.

> *Colossians 3:3 (NLT)*
> *3 For you died to this life, and your real life is hidden with Christ in God.*

OBSCURITY DEFINED
STAGES OF PROCESS AFTER SALVATION

- STAGE 1: Uncovering (Dark to Light): the purpose of that season is doing the work of becoming a new creature, letting go of the past, receiving the love of Christ, and allowing the power of his word to define your new identity in him. In uncovering comes healing and restoration of your soul because in order for you to receive what God has for you, even through prophecy, the soil of your heart must be tended to so that it can fall on fertile ground to produce a harvest.
- STAGE 2: Discovery (Seeking to Know): the purpose is to be transformed and converted by the renewing of your mind and allowing God to change the way you think. In the place of discovery, people saw what I didn't see at first, I could receive, but I couldn't agree because I had not become one with Him yet.
- STAGE 3: Obscurity (Becoming): the purpose is to become what has already been revealed, and you are an active participant in the development and training to become skillful in that. Organize your life, develop the soul to maintain your calling, and study your calling.

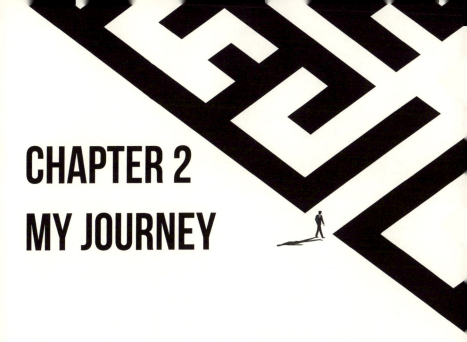

CHAPTER 2
MY JOURNEY

In 2022, I was led by the Holy Spirit to leave my church and join another ministry under the leadership of my Apostle that I had been consistently tuning into his bible studies for about two years. At the time, I had already asked my Apostle to be my mentor while still a member of my former church. Who you are connected to does matter to your journey in God, which is why you must value when he highlights covenant relationships and destiny helpers in your life; they will only appear when you are ready. We do not get to choose the spiritual coverings, churches, and mentors we desire. These people and places are assigned by God, which is why you need discernment and the ability to choose God's purpose over your preference. We must remember that God is guiding us and giv-

"Choose God's purpose over your preference"

ing us things we need along the journey from a finished work perspective, meaning there are things and places God has designed for us to do, and he has already written out the way to get you there. All he needs is your submission, surrender, and agreement; all these require for you to let go and trust the author and finisher of your life and faith.

At my old church, I was just ordained as a Minister, and I was leading the youth dance ministry. At the time, I felt like I was finally coming into who I was for God. And then he called me to transition, and I just couldn't understand because I felt like everything I was doing for God was ending. My function and my flow were all ending, and I felt unfulfilled. I wasn't writing as much, had no opportunities to teach or preach, and I was no longer dancing, but I knew in me the desire, passions, and gifts God had given me. So I decided to pursue opportunities to join dance companies and teach dance on my own but every time I got close to beginning the opportunity they all kept falling through, or I was instructed by God to not go forth. This season literally felt like my life, my will, my timeline, and my passions were all dying, and it hurt so bad and made no sense to me, but even in this, I decided to let go and submit to what God was doing and choose to surrender my plan in order to have his without having full proof or details of how it would work out.

After obeying God to transition ministries, I remember feeling like I knew who I was in God and wondered when my time would come, and then the Holy Spirit responded to this ignorant and zealous thought, saying, "you don't live or act like you know who you are. You live aim-

MY JOURNEY

lessly with no intention or discipline with time; you don't guard your mind and heart like you know who you are, you don't take responsibility for spiritual and natural disciplines that are aligned with who you are." This hard truth helped me realize that you don't wait to get there to act the part; you have to become first before entering into the place you know God has called you to be.

The destination isn't the ultimate goal; your becoming is. You become fit for God's use before you get there!

> *"The destination isn't the ultimate goal; your becoming is."*

Letting my gifts die and feel buried for a season was for me to see the value in my identity as a daughter; it was no longer based on my works and what I can produce in human efforts and reasoning but on who I am and showing up as that being is what pleases God, I was going from dependence on myself and me striving to please God in my human efforts, to learning that it will take full reliance on Him to do anything he has called me to do. Before Jesus started ministry, the father said, "this is my beloved son whom I am well pleased." The beginning of coming into God's calling and destiny is the proper understanding of who you are, and knowing that you bring joy and pleasure to God just by being you. When making the bold decision to transition ministries, my Apostle encouraged me by telling me that "my gifts and functions weren't ending for good but that it would come back with greater power and potency." This really kept me because I knew that there was a limit to my function when operating at my previous ministry, and I was after something greater, the real supernatural, and I realized that it requires more process. So I had to submit my giftings, my desire to be used by God for more private development, which would consist of me becoming one with Abba to look like him and have his character and fruit of the spirit and also to get a greater understanding of my personal assignment because I had the functions and the giftings but not much instruction of the how, why or when what God invested in me would be needed in the earth. I was after what Jesus had, which was power and demonstration. Now I understand that I had the gifts, but God's voiceprint, presence, and potency weren't always on it. There was no backing, just words, no demonstrations or power/authority. Jesus had a life of ministry that was followed by power and demonstration; this should also be our aim.

1 Corinthians 2: 4-6 (AMPC)
4 And my language and my message were not set forth in persuasive (enticing and plausible) words of wisdom, but they were in demonstration of the [Holy] Spirit and power [[a]a proof by the Spirit and power of God, operating on me and stirring in the minds of my hearers the most holy emotions and thus persuading them],
5 So that your faith might not rest in the wisdom of men (human philosophy), but in the power of God.
6 Yet when we are among the full-grown (spiritually mature Christians who are ripe in understanding), we do impart a [higher] wisdom (the knowledge of the divine plan previously hidden); but it is indeed not a wisdom of this present age,

> *or of this world, nor of the leaders and rulers of this age, who are being brought to nothing and are doomed to pass away.*
> *Matthew 7: 28 - 29 (AMPC)*
> *28 When Jesus had finished these sayings [the Sermon on the Mount], the crowds were astonished and overwhelmed with bewildered wonder at His teaching,*
> *29 For He was teaching as One Who had [and was] authority, and not as [did] the scribes.*

The word authority in the Greek "exousia" means force, capacity, competency, and delegated influence. I knew what I had at my old ministry was good enough for then, but not forever. That is the question we must ask ourselves when we are desiring to be used by God, do you want to be short-lived or have longevity in Christ? Longevity requires process, and when it seems like it is taking a long time and others are passing you by, you have to remember that you are being built to last and that the greatest aim should be to know Christ. Paul had to come to this decision when he was faced with the option of holding onto his religious resume of actions he had done in the past or letting it all go to learn and gain Christ in a new way.

> *Philippians 3: 7-11 (NLT)*
> *7 I once thought these things were valuable, but now I consider them worthless because of what Christ has done.*
> *8 Yes, everything else is worthless when compared with the infinite value of knowing Christ Jesus my Lord. For his sake I have discarded everything else, counting it all as garbage,*

so that I could gain Christ 9 and become one with him. I no longer count on my own righteousness through obeying the law; rather, I become righteous through faith in Christ.[c] For God's way of making us right with himself depends on faith. 10 I want to know Christ and experience the mighty power that raised him from the dead. I want to suffer with him, sharing in his death, 11 so that one way or another, I will experience the resurrection from the dead!

In obscurity, you come to know him, which was Paul's aim. Paul decided to count all the things he did as worthless so that he may know Christ. Knowledge of him is what I need because I operate through him and boast about what he has already done for me. It is valuable to gain Christ and become one with him instead of counting on your own works of righteousness. We are righteous through faith in God; this is the new covenant. Paul wanted to know Christ and experience the power that raised him from the dead and suffer with him so he could experience resurrection power. This is the heart of the covenant, the heartbeat, and the value system of those in the covenant. This is not a place Paul arrived at but he made it his greatest aim. Once I understood this value system of the covenant, I began to understand the value of obscurity. I was at a place where my gifts were identified, affirmed, and developed, but I wasn't, I didn't learn or have knowledge of the soul needed and the lifestyle required in order to fulfill my calling or purpose. Obscurity was the place where I would learn these things.

CHAPTER 3
SIGNS OF OBSCURITY

O ne of the main reasons I came to Christ was because I wanted to find meaning to my life, I wanted fulfillment, and I wanted to understand why I was created because throughout life, I experienced pain, and my trauma was all I could see, which led to a silent battle of depression and suicidal thoughts. I truly desired to know the purpose of my life because I was hurting so much that I entertained the thoughts of the enemy to take my life. My pain was a part of my identity; it was my baggage I carried around silently, trying to hide but also secretly wanting someone to see and discern it through the manifestations produced through my actions and behaviors. I came to Christ to find meaning. I came to Christ because his love for me showed me that I was worth it. His love confronted the brokenness, hurt, rejection, and low self-esteem. His love was the answer to my cry for acceptance, validation, and attention that had developed through childhood experiences.

As I began to surrender my life to Christ, he began to transform me and send prophetic words through people, which brought clarity and created a place where God's plan could manifest in my life. So being called out and acknowledged in church made me feel great about myself, it made me feel important, it made me feel worth it and seen. People began to call out and notice my giftings, and this was even more exciting, I was on a journey to discovering who I was, but I only knew it because it was spoken over my life. I had not yet stepped into agreement with the word because I didn't see what others saw, because my personal view of myself was still blurred and broken.

So as I began to learn about myself and people that saw who God saw would call it out of me, it would bring clarity and direction, but it also fed a deep place and void of insecurity manifesting as a desire to be seen, acknowledged and accepted. Especially when using the gift of dance God gave me, the stage was my safe place, and it was a place where all my hard work of training and practice shined and was acknowledged and rewarded. So I began to strive to be used by God, desire for my giftings to be used because it made me feel effective, it made me feel important, it made me feel like I was finally enough, it made me feel like I was better because in my head I equated public demonstration of a gift to intimacy and closeness with the father. I later learned that gifts and calling come without repentance, meaning you could be doing things for God and in the name of God but never be known by him. We must realize that before God desires to use us for his glory, he desires to have our hearts and unbroken fellowship with us, which is developed by growing a right relationship with him.

> *Romans 11:29 (KJV)*
> *29 For the gifts and calling of God are without repentance.*
> *Matthew 7: 21-23 (NKJV)*
> *21 "Not everyone who says to Me, 'Lord, Lord,' shall enter the kingdom of heaven, but he who does the will of My Father in heaven. 22 Many will say to Me in that day, 'Lord, Lord, have we not prophesied in Your name, cast out demons in Your name, and done many wonders in Your name?' 23 And then I will declare to them, 'I never knew you; depart from Me, you who practice lawlessness!'*

Through submitting to obscurity, I have come to realize that the priority should not be your giftedness being put on display, but what really counts is knowing Christ. Because you can be used and still depressed and still bound by things from your past because this deliverance is only obtained and maintained by drawing near to Abba and developing a relationship with him. You can be used and have no knowledge of your identity, which leads to living a life below what God intended because identity is the place where DNA, inheritance, and authority comes from knowing who you are and knowing what you have access to. Healing from rejection and low self-esteem came from knowing that I please God because of who I am and not what I can do for him. Through growing my relationship with God, I learned that he is not like a man; I don't have to work to earn his love because it was already given before I decided to turn to him.Obscurity is important because God needs to deal with your character, check your motives, and make sure they are pure and are coming from a healed and whole place.

> *Hebrews 4: 12 (NLT)*
> *12 For the word of God is alive and powerful. It is sharper than the sharpest two-edged sword, cutting between soul and spirit, between joint and marrow. It exposes our innermost thoughts and desires.*

It was in the place of obscurity that I realized my motive for being used was off because it was feeling a void where I enjoyed receiving the glory, instead of giving it to God. When you are hidden in him, people should only see him, and when people praise you, it is your job to say it was him because you know it was only by his grace, and this takes humility. This is why God was able to trust Daniel with elevation and the kings of cities because he had proved that when man pointed these supernatural abilities to Daniel, he would always make sure the glory was directed towards God and not himself. There is a treasure in us and an empowering agent, which is the Holy Ghost, which is the spirit of God that was given to us, that leads and guides us into all truth, and is our helper and gives us the ability to fulfill our calling.

> *Daniel 2: 27-28 (NKJV)*
> *27 Daniel answered in the presence of the king and said, "The secret which the king hath demanded, the wise men, the astrologers, the magicians, and the soothsayers cannot show unto the king.*

28 But there is a God in heaven who revealeth secrets, and maketh known to King Nebuchadnezzar what shall be in the latter days. Thy dream and the visions of thy head upon thy bed are these:

2 Corinthians 4:7 (NLT)
7 We now have this light shining in our hearts, but we ourselves are like fragile clay jars containing this great treasure. This makes it clear that our great power is from God, not from ourselves.

Obscurity is when you know there is a leader in you, but you are currently in a position where you are serving another man's vision. Obscurity can feel like "I know I have the gift to teach, so when others teach, I wonder why I am not getting chosen." Obscurity is the place where you are aware of your functions, gifts, and calling, but you are in a place of training, so most of your work seems private, but it's because you are building with God. You tend to feel hidden in public settings. It's like you are aware of who you are but see no current manifestation of it. This can be part of development when you begin to lose faith and interest and allow the enemy access to seduce you out of divine process and pattern because you are still being led by your own passion. Obscurity runs through every part of your soul, which can be a place where the enemy can ensnare you because it was not dealt with. Just because God has made an announcement over you doesn't mean it is time. He tells you before so you can prepare, so you can adjust your life disciplines to align with who you are and what you will do. Sometimes, we know who we are, but we still have not brought our lifestyle to align with that truth. Being hidden brought up a lot for me in my soul; in moments when the spirit would be moving in a service and using a particular person to flow prophetically, I would find myself

"Sometimes, we know who we are, but we still have not brought our lifestyle to align with that truth"

getting jealous, angry, and comparing myself to others; it made me evaluate if I am doing all the right things to qualify to be used, I began to question is their prayer life better than mines? It made me feel like I was not worth it; it made me feel like I was not enough, which were all thoughts I had believed in in the past. The enemy will always try to repaint a narrative you have experienced before to trigger those same emotions of insecurity and disbelief. This is why self-awareness is important: The enemy studies us and knows our weaknesses, but we have to be aware of those places as well and develop disciplines to conquer them for good. Our emotional "triggers" will always be places where the enemy has the advantage unless we do the work to conquer our souls.

Obscurity brought up self-righteous thoughts when I would compare myself to "fresh babes in Christ or in my opinion, not righteous enough people " being used. It was not just being used but also people who seemed to be in the spotlight, on the pulpit, with a microphone. Maybe I am just not called to flow in that way; it is the lie I would settle for in order to escape my feelings of rejection, disappointment, and frustration. Many times, we try to find a valid reason to explain our feelings in order to escape the overwhelming and frustrating experience of feeling them. I would rationalize many ideas in my head of why I was not being used in the way I saw God use others instead of building my faith and expectation for God to do the same in my life. These experiences were frustrating because I felt greatness on the inside of me, but I didn't see it manifested externally. I was frustrated with where I was because I knew there was more to me. And I wanted others to see it, too, because there is still a part of me that is insecure and looking for affirmation. I wanted people to know and see me, but I didn't even know or see me in its fullness yet. I've learned that before God could use me, he had to purify and correct my motives. God truly does his best work from the inside out.

The truth was I liked the attention of being used by God, but I realized that if God used me before confronting pride and self-righteousness, I would be used with the wrong heart posture. God using me to do good works would make me feel like I am doing all the right things to please him, which is why he can pick me. But this places the focus again on my work when really the truth is the holy spirit can choose to use anyone; it is out of our control. So, being used by God does not mean you are pleasing him; being used by God doesn't necessarily mean that he knows you. Being used doesn't mean that you have intimacy with God. Being used without intimacy with God is a recipe for disaster because when the trails of life come, you breakdown because you have not made God your firm foundation or vital necessity. You can not build your spiritual walk with God based on a gift; you must build it on a relationship and fellowship led by love for God and a desire to know him.

This relationship with God will then change your perspective from being used by God to partnering with Him.I would always tell myself that I think I know who I am, but I have not had the life-defining moment my Apostle would share about how God took him to heaven and manteled him with prayer and was told to build a house of prayer and raise prophetic intercessors. We all need this moment, though, because we need to know our distinction and our assignment so we stay in alignment and don't get discouraged when we see others building differently. These encounters are in obscurity, and are a direct result of seeking these things out. The secret to remaining persistent in your seek is having the faith and expectation that God's word is true; if you seek, you shall find. (Matthew 7:7)

As you think about people in the Bible who knew God, their knowledge of God is what kept them in the storm and trail. Could it be that the reason you are fainting is because you don't really know the God you serve? You just know how to be used? Your gift shouldn't lead you because there will be moments where being "busy" doing ministry can be used as a distraction when God is leading you another way, but you can not see it because your desire to flaunt your gift and perfect your gift is much greater than intimacy with Abba.I have learned that these feelings I was experiencing were not something I was supposed to rationalize on my own but things that I needed to bring to God. In vulnerability, it was only at this moment that I admitted to God what I was experiencing emotionally he begin to reveal to me the season I was encountering which was obscurity. It was a hard season because I finally got to the point in my life where I believed that there was greatness inside of me and that there was a call on my life and I was eager to respond because I began to see it and feel it for myself. I was growing in my confidence and ability to be used for his glory, but I did not realize that reaching that point was my pre-requisite for the season of obscurity.

Being hidden revealed so much about the state of my soul that I would have never known was there void of encountering this season. Being hidden killed all selfish ambition and pushed me to build a relationship of unbroken fellowship with God based on love and a true desire to know him. Obscurity is a place of discovery and awakening of gifts and callings you may not know are there, a place where you become and develop your calling and become skillful in the anointing and, most importantly, where you become one with the father and you look more like him, because when people see you they should see Christ. When you confront the enemies of where God has sent you, you can not show up as yourself, but you must show up as your divine self which is Christ in you.

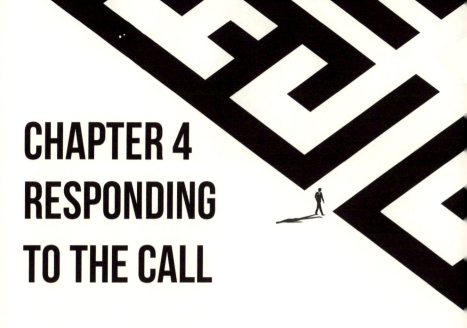

CHAPTER 4
RESPONDING TO THE CALL

> *2 Peter 1:3 (NLT)*
> *3 By his divine power, God has given us everything we need for living a godly life. We have received all of this by coming to know him, the one who called us to himself by means of his marvelous glory and excellence.*

The great and most assuring thing about being called by God to fulfill a purpose and assignment is knowing that he didn't leave you on earth alone to fulfill it, but he has given you his spirit, the holy spirit, which is your empowering agent in navigating life, skillfully functioning in your gifts, and fulfilling your purpose. Remember, we have been given all we need to live a Godly life. We must understand the importance of developing a relationship with the person of the Holy Spirit that lives on the inside of us and serves as our guide and much more. Here are a few ways you can expect the Holy Spirit to reveal himself in your daily life as you yield to Him and make space for Him to come in.

> ## Romans 8: 13-14 (AMPC)
> *13 For if you live according to [the dictates of] the flesh, you will surely die. But if through the power of the [Holy] Spirit you are [habitually] putting to death (making extinct, deadening) the [evil] deeds prompted by the body, you shall [really and genuinely] live forever.14 For all who are led by the Spirit of God are sons of God*

PURPOSE OF THE HOLY SPIRIT

- **TO LEAD:** John 16: 13 (AMPC)

13 But when He, the Spirit of Truth (the Truth-giving Spirit), comes, He will guide you into all the Truth (the whole, full Truth). For He will not speak His own message [on His own authority], but He will tell whatever He hears [from the Father; He will give the message that has been given to Him], and He will announce and declare to you the things that are to come [that will happen in the future].

- **TO TEACH AND COMFORT:** John 14:26 (AMPC)

26 But the Comforter (Counselor, Helper, Intercessor, Advocate, Strengthener, Standby), the Holy Spirit, Whom the Father will send in My name [in My place, to represent Me and act on My behalf], He will teach you all things. And He will cause you to recall (will remind you of, bring to your remembrance) everything I have told you.

RESPONDING TO THE CALL

- **TO DISTRIBUTE GIFTS & DIVINE TECHNOLOGIES:** 1 Corinthians 12:11 (NLT)

11 It is the one and only Spirit who distributes all these gifts. He alone decides which gift each person should have.

Acts 2:17 (NLT)

17 'In the last days,' God says, 'I will pour out my Spirit upon all people. Your sons and daughters will prophesy. Your young men will see visions, and your old men will dream dreams.

- **TO PRODUCE FRUIT:** Galatians 5: 22-23 (NLT)

22 But the Holy Spirit produces this kind of fruit in our lives: love, joy, peace, patience, kindness, goodness, faithfulness, 23 gentleness, and self-control. There is no law against these things!

2 Timothy 1:7 (NLT)

7 For God has not given us a spirit of fear and timidity, but of power, love, and self-discipline.

You will come to learn of the Holy Spirit as all of these things when you develop a life of fellowship with Him. This can be developed through abiding with God, meditating on his word, praying in the spirit daily, and making a conscious decision to let the spirit be in the lead of your life, which is a sign of spiritual maturity.

When God called Moses (Exodus 3: 7-12), he first got his attention, then he shared a problem in the world and his intended solution, which was to come down and deliver the Israelites from bondage. Moses' response to the call of God was what if they don't believe me. Moses was really saying "God I don't believe you in me either. I will go with uncertainty, and they will pick this up; I am fearful that if people ask about the God I serve, I will have nothing to say because I have no experience with you. I am still coming into believing you for myself." So God revealed himself. Moses desired to know God beyond his encounter; he wanted to know who was sending him and the God that would be with him. Moses had many excuses as to why he could not go; this is because he did not realize that it wasn't based on his human abilities and efforts, but the only way he would be successful was for him to have the understanding that God was with him and he was coming down to earth through him and all he needed was his cooperation and obedience to show up as God in the earth. When God calls us, he will always show us who He is and who we are by correcting any false narratives we may believe about ourselves and brings us back to the original intent of existence; he then reveals a problem and the solution and equips you to be the solutionist because that is where prosperity comes from.

> *Jeremiah 29:11 (KJV)*
> *11 For I know the thoughts that I think toward you, saith the LORD, thoughts of peace, and not of evil, to give you an expected end.*

This is a very familiar scripture, and in the season of obscurity, you must use it as a reminder and encouragement that God's thoughts towards you are good and full of peace and prosperity, and this truth gives you hope in the final outcome. I learned to submit to obscurity because I realized that God had given me a glance at my final outcome

RESPONDING TO THE CALL

by allowing me to see and hear about all I was to become, but I had to submit to obscurity to get a greater understanding of who I am and why I am so I can do it skillfully and boldly because the more I know about who God called me to be the more effective I can be at fulfilling my part in the body of Christ. When I get a greater understanding of who I am, I can become a specialist at who I was created to be and not fall into the trap of comparing myself to others, which is rooted in an insecurity of self. Who you are is worth learning about and becoming, and what you are

"Who you are is worth learning about and becoming, and what you are called to do is worth investigating"

called to do is worth investigating. The season of obscurity is an essential part of the journey of fulfilling purpose. This process should not be skipped but should be discerned and submitted to because it is the key to going from potential to promise. Obscurity is important because you should not approach any assignment without proper preparation and training. You need to be mature in your calling, instead of flowing prematurely because, in this season, you will learn how to live the lifestyle that helps you maintain your calling, because there is a soul and a lifestyle you must have in order to fulfill your purpose. God's processing reminds me of any career you desire to pursue in the world. There is a training process. For example, in order to become a doctor, you must first go to medical school, where you learn a lot of information about all the different types of functions in the field, and you take a bunch of tests to prove your mastery of

31

knowledge. Next, you go into residency or internship which is when you practice all you have learned in your specified place of practice so you are now becoming more specialized and given the ability to practice medicine and become skillful through your experiences. Then, after residency, you become a licensed doctor with the ability to open your own practice. Obscurity is that place of residency or internship because it's the place where you are developing in the specified places of your calling and gifts that God has revealed and anointed you for. Your first anointing, announcement, or acknowledgement is not the release to operate in it, but it is for you to allow the seed of what has been planted in you to grow and develop.

It's almost like you just found out that you're pregnant and expecting a baby; you begin to show, but it's not time to give birth until the full 9 months of growth is over. During that 9 months of preparation, you find out about what and who you are carrying, and you begin to make life adjustments to cultivate a safe and efficient place for your baby to grow. You prepare your home for this new living being you are about to bring into the world; it's like you are birthing a new part of who you are. This is the same as our callings and gifts. We have to allow them to process in and through us and allow them to organize our lives for us, purge, heal, and restore our souls, and get experience in it to grow in it. Sometimes, this experience looks like serving in another man's vision or ministry to learn and be cultivat-

"Serving builds humility, and it gives you the opportunity to sharpen your gifting and become"

ed. There is so much value in serving; serving builds humility, and it gives you the opportunity to sharpen your gifting and become. The Lord has been so intentional in the places and people he has given me the opportunity to serve. While serving, I've grown and become more skillful in my gifting, and I have learned so much wisdom from someone who has already gone through the process of obscurity. While serving you have to be willing to wait until God's appointed time and build the heart of a servant, which is something Jesus taught his disciples. (Matthew 23:11-12)

The season of obscurity timeline can be different for all because our relationship and journey with God is personal. Your season of obscurity is up when God says so because you only need to show up when what you have been carrying and mastering is needed in the world. So you may be hidden only because your time to be revealed to the world has not come; this is why stewarding this season is so important because when the time comes, you can't be trying to get ready. You will already be ready, and because you were patient in the process you have longevity and what you release also has the backing of heaven with you because you have truly become one with God. Your first aim in your response to the call of God on your life is to become one with Him. Come to a place where there is oneness in your heart, soul, and mind, which then impacts what you believe and what is spoken out of your mouth.

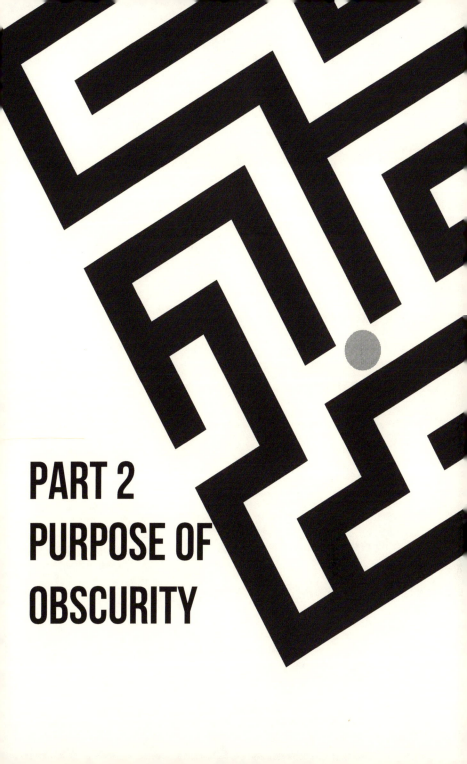

PART 2
PURPOSE OF
OBSCURITY

CHAPTER 5
THE POWER OF
OBSCURITY

> *Isaiah 49: 1-2 (KJV)*
> *1 Listen, O isles, unto me; and hearken, ye people, from far; The LORD hath called me from the womb; from the bowels of my mother hath he made mention of my name. 2 And he hath made my mouth like a sharp sword; in the shadow of his hand hath he hid me and made me a polished shaft; in his quiver hath he hid me.*

The prophet Isaiah understood the power and the purpose of being hidden by God. Isaiah understood that from the womb, there was a calling on his life. He understood that the first step to fulfill this calling was for him to be hidden in the shadow of God's hand, which symbolizes protection and intimacy with God. In this place, God made his mouth like a sharp sword, which symbolizes God filling his mouth with the word of God because the word of God is a sharp sword.

> *Hebrews 4:12 (NLT)*
>
> *12 For the word of God is alive and powerful. It is sharper than the sharpest two-edged sword, cutting between soul and spirit, between joint and marrow. It exposes our innermost thoughts and desires.*

In order for the word to get in Isaiah's mouth, it had to get in his heart, which happens when you allow God to water the soil of your heart with the word of God. The internal work of the heart is vital in determining what comes out of your mouth and the revelation you have of the word. In the hand of God is where Isaiah became a cutting instrument for God to use. Next, Isaiah was hidden in God's quiver, which is a place for arrows to be used as weapons. God made him into a polished shaft, which is a process of purification by testing and proving. Being hidden in God's quiver is a place for equipping and training based on your specific calling. Your first calling is to be all His; the next step is to become that which he originated you to be from the beginning.Isaiah was forced into hiding to be made a sharp shooting weapon for God, which is what God desires for all of his people to do. After God reveals the parts of your identity and calling, it is your job to seek it out and develop the lifestyle to carry it out. Every prophetic word God has spoken concerning you must be sought out; when you seek Him, you get understanding.

> *Proverbs 25:2 (AMPC)*
>
> *2 It is the glory of God to conceal a thing, but the glory of kings is to search out a thing.*

THE POWER OF OBSCURITY

Conceal here in the Greek means " to hide oneself, to be hidden, be concealed, to hide carefully." Here we see that God conceals things for kings to search them out. Meaning it is hidden for a certain type of person to find. That king symbolizes us as the offspring of the Godhead, to whom the mysterious and hidden things of God belong, but they will only be revealed or accessed by those who seek them out. Setting yourself to seek God takes patience, humility, submission, and persistence in seeking. It is done in obscurity. Without Christ, this place feels like rejection, but with Christ, it is preserved protection.

Obscurity is the place where you are aware that there is greatness inside of you. You may have had glimpses of God's ability to use you, but you still have not sat with God long enough to grasp the entirety of who you are. If you are not able to articulate it fully or clearly, then there is more seeking you need to do. If your gift and passions are all that excite you, you will be drawn to places and things that affirm that but don't develop that or you. You have to know and value the process of becoming, so you can resist the desire for public praise in exchange for private or obscure development. So it may look like people are passing you by, and you may be looking to be acknowledged, but you must realize that at some point in your walk with the Lord, you have to stop waiting for man to tell you who you are and go to God to get the intel.

> *"You have to know and value the process of becoming, so you can resist the desire for public praise in exchange for private development."*

Obscurity teaches you how to clothe yourself with humility, and reveals how much pride resides in your heart. It allowed me to face the questions of "How do you respond when it's not you but them in the spotlight? How do you act when you are not in the front, or all eyes are not on you, and you receive no applause?" If the place of obscurity bothers you or makes you feel not good enough or worth it, it is a soul hole that needs to be healed and given a different narrative. You may be going from church to church, place to place, conference to conference, looking for someone to tell you who you are. But when will you know for yourself? Who are you outside of what you can do and your giftings? If you do not know, then this is found in obscurity.

Obscurity is a dark place, so it may feel discouraging and like nothing is happening, but little is much in the hands of the potter; you just have to be willing to trust his plan and know he is leading you on the best path possible, even if it seems to be taking longer. Obscurity can be an exciting place because it is the place and opportunity for God to encounter you personally. When you have an encounter for yourself, no one will be able to move you because you have been established by God, and the Holy Ghost can always remind you, because what you know about yourself is no longer something you have heard about, but you have now gained revelation for yourself and that has produced the faith needed to partner with God to fulfill everything he has said. Your boldness comes from your encounter

"Obscurity can be an exciting place because it is the place and opportunity for God to encounter you personally"

THE POWER OF OBSCURITY

with God, not from the affirmation or validation of others.

Obscurity feels like a potter's wheel, turning around and around in circles, but it's because you are on his wheel, being made fit for his use. In order to navigate obscurity, you must adjust your mindset to the truth, " this isn't a unnessary cycle; I am on the potter's wheel being molded and made fit for God's use.

> *2 Timothy 2: 20-21 (KJV)*
> *20 But in a great house, there are not only vessels of gold and of silver, but also of wood and of earth; and some to honour, and some to dishonour. 21 If a man therefore purge himself from these, he shall be a vessel unto honour, sanctified, and meet for the master's use, and prepared unto every good work.*

Obscurity is a place of discovery and awakening for you and a place where you become and develop your calling. Your calling is who you are, and it has to be discovered and developed. Your gifting is what you do, your operation, and your function, and this must be awakened or endowed and then made skillful through yielding to the Holy Spirit. Obscurity is important because you must become the person who can house your calling and develop the lifestyle and consecration to God that will maintain and sustain you. Obscurity is a time when you learn to build your prayer life, yield to the holy spirit, and work to become skillful in your giftings and anointing.

CHAPTER 6
LIVING A LIFE
WORTHY OF THE CALL

> *Ephesians 4:1-2 (TPT)*
> *1 As a prisoner of the Lord, I plead with you to walk holy, in a way that is suitable to your high rank, given to you in your divine calling. 2With tender humility and quiet patience, always demonstrate gentleness and generous love toward one another, especially toward those who may try your patience.*

In the book of Ephesians, Apostle Paul urges believers to cultivate a lifestyle and character that aligns with their new life in Christ. He also highlights the mystery of our identity in Christ, which must be something we believe because it plays a major role in how we approach and navigate life. The Bible instructs us to walk out our own soul salvation; this means that yes, we are saved by grace, the old life has passed away, and all things are made new, but there is work we must do in order to become who we already are in Christ, knowing that it is already done gives us the faith, hope, and endurance to go after it. Ephesians 4: 17-32 outlines the new life we must live and how there should be a clear separation and distinction between our lives and unbelievers. There is a new way of living that Christ has unfolded within you that you must yield to and learn to live from. Every revelation from God should transform you as you learn how to live in union and oneness with him. All of this work should be done in obscurity.

Obscurity is a place of death to the old self and even habits to put on the new self, so it won't be something you just say with your lips but a revelation and truth that has impacted your heart, which transforms the way you live. Many times in religion, there may be the teachings of a man telling you how to live, what to wear, and what to eat, but this only produces many behavior modifiers, which doesn't result in long-lasting converted believers. True conversion and transformation happens as the believer learns of God for themselves, which happens when a daily relationship with God begins. True transformation comes because of man's encounter with God for themselves and not man's encounter with man and their made-up traditions. God's word and power are the only things that can save and transform a person's life, which is what Paul encourages all believers to do in Ephesians.

Titus 1:16 (NLT)
16 Such people claim they know God, but they deny him by the way they live. They are detestable and disobedient, worthless for doing anything good.

Many may claim to know God and even have revelations about what he has called them to do, but they don't live like it. The only thing God has touched is their mouth, but their hearts have still not come into alignment with it. When his word has not gotten into your heart, then it will not change your life, this is why our hearts must be guarded because this is where our life flows from (Proverbs 4: 23).This shows that in order for our life to change, our hearts must change; the only way for the heart to change is to let the word of God enter it and allow it to transform you and renew your mind after the ways of Christ.Paul then writes to Timothy, his spiritual son and apostolic apprentice, instructions on how to live a life worthy of his calling and how to carry God's message to nations just like him. Timothy traveled with Paul on his missionary journeys and was later entrusted with a similar responsibility of his own. These were stages of preparation in obscurity for Timothy.

> *2 Timothy 2:22 (NLT)*
> *22 Run from anything that stimulates youthful lusts. Instead, pursue righteous living, faithfulness, love, and peace. Enjoy the companionship of those who call on the Lord with pure hearts.*

Paul instructed Timothy to run from anything that stimulates youthful lust. Lusts here in Greek is epithymía, meaning a longing, desire, craving, especially for what is forbidden. In our world today, the response to this instruction can be different because we all may have had different pasts and things in our youth that stimulated lifestyles and habits of sin that are no longer beneficial to our new life in

Christ. There will be things in your walk that may not be considered a sin, but they may be unfruitful to your walk with Christ. The Bible tells us that we are the righteousness of Christ, and so we must pursue a lifestyle of holiness and consecration unto the Lord.

In my own journey with Christ, one thing that I had to flee from and give up entirely was alcohol. I remember when I first gave my life to Christ in my freshman year of college, there came a time where the Lord delivered me from the desire to consume hard liquor and alcohol and drunkenness. So I transitioned to lighter libations and wine, and it was just my norm to drink whenever I felt like it or special celebratory occasions in my adulthood. I honestly found nothing wrong with it because my intention behind drinking was no longer the same. I wasn't trying to numb anything to escape from the pain the trauma in my life had caused. I simply would drink because it was enjoyable, to relax or relieve stress that I may have encountered as an educator. There came a time in my walk with God when the Lord told me to let it go. It was such a clear instruction that I will never forget that encounter. I had gotten up for my daily devotion with the Lord, and before I could get deep into my worship and communion with Him, the Holy Spirit instructed me to pour out all the wine I had just brought the night before, before I could proceed in engaging the father. I mean, I wrestled with God for a minute with this instruction by asking him questions about the time limit of this instruction or if it would be forever, he never really answered that request at that moment, but I knew there was such an urgency that was required to my response to this instruction so I obeyed, and ever since that moment, I have never drank again simply because God said so and he led me to his word to back it up. I realized that it was a personal conviction to my consecration to the Lord, and I came to a point of maturity in my walk where I wanted Jesus more than to enjoy that pleasure of life. There are things we are free to do that will not send us to hell, but they still are not profitable to us; I believe these sacrifices can only be made because of your love for the father being ranked higher than any other thing from the earth.

Ephesians 5:18 (NLT)
18 Don't be drunk with wine, because that will ruin your life. Instead, be filled with the Holy Spirit.

1 Corinthians 10: 23 (NLT)
23 You say, "I am allowed to do anything,"—but not everything is good for you. You say, "I am allowed to do anything,"—but not everything is beneficial.

Because I was one bound by my craving and addiction to alcohol, I did see that the impact on my life was not profitable. Moments of drunkenness would always lead to sexual immorality and/or more lust for other things; it gave me an excuse for wild living, which no longer aligned with the lifestyle of my new identity in Christ. In obscurity is where we put to death certain things that no longer serve our identity in Christ, and you must remember that certain instructions from God don't always deserve an explanation, but it does deserve your obedience. Our obedience to God stems from a place of love and relationship with him, just

NAVIGATING OBSCURITY

like our relationships on earth; when we love someone, we tend to do our best to make sure that we change or stop anything that may cause a hindrance to our love and relationship we must have this same heart posture and mindset in our relationship with Christ knowing that he will not withhold any good thing us, knowing that his discipline is for our good and for our benefit because he has things and prosperous plans for us that can only be released and obtained by doing things his way.

In 2 Timothy, Paul imparts wisdom and some great lessons he has gained from experience to encourage Timothy in his own ministry. In this place of obscurity, it may look like you are receiving knowledge, training, and wisdom from God-sent mentors and leaders while also serving them, and this is all a part of God's plan of processing his people. So you can change your perspective of this place of obscurity. You are not stuck or behind schedule, but in fact, this is your perfect time to make investments in your now, for the future God has built for you to enter later. We must understand that no time or season in the will of God is wasted time. You must discern the times and gain an understanding of its purpose so you can see the value of it and embrace it while you are in it. I know your belly is leaping every time you see someone doing or flowing in the call, gifting, career, or position you see yourself becoming. I know you may feel hidden or behind time serving another man's vision while also having one of your own, and you may wonder when your time will

> *"We must understand that no time or season in the will of God is wasted time"*

LIVING A LIFE WORTHY OF THE CALL

come, but you must discipline yourself to focus on God's intention for now instead of what you see him doing for you later. In these moments, the key is stewardship, stewarding every word, idea, business plan, position, and solution that God has given you because when the proper time presents itself, God intends for you to be ready and well-equipped for every good work, he assigns you too.

KEYS FROM PAUL TO TIMOTHY IN OBSCURITY

- Stir up and guard the gift imparted to you
- Overcome every evil with the power of God as a victorious soldier of Christ.
- Divorce yourself from the distractions of the world to fully satisfy God.
- Live your life empowered by the grace of God which is found in union with him.
- Deposit what I have taught you to others.
- Make Jesus your aim and focus in life and ministry.
- Always be ready to present yourself as a perfect and mature minister who can rightly explain the word of truth.
- Avoid false teachings, empty chatter, worthless words, and immature arguments.
- Be a pure container of Christ dedicated to the honorable purposes of God.
- Flee from all ambitions and lusts of youth and chase purity and whatever builds your faith.
- Have great patience towards the immature, and be gentle and skilled in helping others see the truth.
- Stay away from people who pretend to have respect and love for God but, in reality, want nothing to do with his

power and who are forever learning but never coming into the knowledge of truth

- Continue to advance in strength with the truth wrapped around your heart because God has taught you this himself

---

Paul then speaks of Timothy's loyalty to him and his ministry because Timothy modeled his life after the love and endurance Paul demonstrated in his ministry.

> ## 2 Timothy 3: 10-11 (TPT)
>
> 10 " But you, Timothy, have closely followed my example and the truth that I've imparted to you. You have modeled your life after the love and endurance I've demonstrated in my ministry by not giving up. The faith I have, you now have. What I have hungered for in life has now become your longing as well. The patience I have with others, you now demonstrate. 11 And the same persecutions and difficulties I have endured, you have also endured. Yes, you know all about what I had to suffer while in Antioch, Iconium, and Lystra. You're aware of all the persecution I endured there; yet the Lord delivered me from every single one of them!"

Paul's final instructions were to proclaim the Word of God and stand up for it no matter what. Preach when it's convenient and when it's not. Preach with the full expression of the Holy Spirit with wisdom and patience as you instruct people. He tells him to carry in his heart the passion of his calling as a church planter, to keep a clear conscience, to not be afraid of suffering, and to fully carry out the ministry God has given to him. These instructions are so pivotal to Timothy's success, and these are things that can be received and learned in obscurity so that you can

LIVING A LIFE WORTHY OF THE CALL

carry out the will of God for your life full term and finish full of faith and joy and with assurance that you did all that God called you to do. This was the confidence that Paul had as his ministry was coming to an end, and Timothy would now continue it on.

The covenant relationship between Paul and Timothy is a perfect example of what obscurity looks like, its purpose, and the responsibilities of the mentor or spiritual covering and the mentee or spiritual child. God does not intend for us to become alone or void of relationships, but he sends us to a church, and gives us destiny helpers and mentors, and we must remain planted and honor them and become who he has called us to be because he has already given you the personalized and intentional environment for you to become. In obscurity, never allow yourself to give into the temptation to disconnect from the place or the people God assigns to your life because they play a vital role in your becoming.

CHAPTER 7
COMPONENTS
OF IDENTITY

I n an earlier chapter, I spoke about one of the main purposes of obscurity, which is to get a full understanding of who you are and the assignment God has for you to fulfill on earth. You must understand that you were not born by accident, but when God sent you from heaven to earth, he was strategic and had an intended purpose for your existence. This truth should free you from all negative narratives that life or even people may have told you. It should take captive every stronghold of shame, lack of confidence and low self-esteem, belief in purpose, rejection, and silence every thought of suicide because the truth that God has a purpose for your life makes you free.

Jeremiah 1: 4- 10 (KJV)
4 The word of the LORD came to me, saying,5 "Before I formed you in the womb I knew[a] you, before you were born I set you apart; I appointed you as a prophet to the

> *nations."6 "Alas, Sovereign LORD," I said, "I do not know how to speak; I am too young."7 But the LORD said to me, "Do not say, 'I am too young.' You must go to everyone I send you to and say whatever I command you. 8 Do not be afraid of them, for I am with you and will rescue you," declares the LORD.9 Then the LORD reached out his hand and touched my mouth and said to me, "I have put my words in your mouth. 10 See, today I appoint you over nations and kingdoms to uproot and tear down, to destroy and overthrow, to build and to plant."*

When God called Jeremiah in his teenage years, God gave Jeremiah all the components of his identity and purpose. I like to break these components up into the five Ws + H, which are who, what, where, when, why and how. These probably look really familiar from your English class in school. These question words are used to allow students, writers, and researchers to understand the full scope of the topic being discussed.

JEREMIAH IDENTITY COMPONENTS

WHO? Set apart, appointed, called to be a Prophet

WHAT? Appointed to stand up against nations and kingdoms.

WHERE? Nations & kingdoms

WHEN? NOW (never say you are too young)

WHY? To stand up and against nations

HOW? I have put my words in your mouth, through seeing you will say. I am with you, and I will take care of you.

After Jeremiah's first calling, God showed him how he would get this assignment done throughout his life. He took Jeremiah through a series of tests to see if he could see with his spiritual sight. He asked him, "Jeremiah, what do you see?" Jeremiah responded correctly and God confirmed that he saw well, which gave him access to more revelation and understanding, allowing him to partner with what God revealed. We can not only seek out why we need to know WHO we are first and then abide in God to get the full components of your identity to allow the fullness of the Godhead to have expression in you. These are the questions you should ask and seek God about in the season of Obscurity because all these instructions must come from him.

COMPONENTS OF IDENTITY

Who AM I? Genetic makeup

Why AM I? Purpose/ Passion

What AM I? Gift, Function, Assignment, Calling

Where Am I? Sphere, Geographical, Realm of Influence

When Am I? Prophetic Timing, Where am I at currently in my walk with you?

How am I? Showing up as your divine self in union with God. Knowing God is with you, yielding to him, and becoming skillful in your calling.

There are certain answers to these questions that will be personal and unique to each person, but overall, we must come to understand that we are sons/daughters of God, and we are his offspring in the earth created for his purpose and to glorify him. Through our purpose and the use of our gifts through surrendering them to him, he empowers and equips us to send us to one or multiple spheres of influence, and at the proper timing, he will call us to come forth and fulfill his plan by showing up as the Christ in us by spending the time to become skillful masters and specialist in what he has graced us to do knowing that we are never alone and wherever he sends us God is with us because everything God calls us to do will need Him. Everything God has called us to do can only be done in and through Him.

If you are missing any of these components, you will be off in your pursuits, prayer, assignments and decisions. This sounds like confusion, frustration, and an unfulfilled life. This is because you have not sat long enough to get the fullness of the Godhead in you. Discerning the will of God for your life is vital to the fulfillment of your life. Your real life is hidden in him, and it's hidden for you to seek out. In obscurity, you come to understand How God expresses himself through you. Why has he chosen you? Why is the spirit of the Lord upon you? Your past experience even begins to make sense in the plan of God, and you begin to see the beauty of how God can make everything work for your good. Our books are already written; we just have to read and seek them out by reading his word. Jesus knew why the spirit of the Lord was upon Him, and he walked the earth with clear intention, focus, direction, and urgency because he knew who he was and why he was sent to earth and he knew who was with him which was God.

> ### Luke 4:18 (NLT)
> 18 The Spirit of the Lord is upon me, for he has anointed me to bring Good News to the poor. He has sent me to proclaim that captives will be released, that the blind will see, that the oppressed will be set free.

When you gain the wisdom and knowledge of your assignment, you come out of the season of Obscurity with a greater sense of clarity and boldness because you know the

COMPONENTS OF IDENTITY

God of your existence, the God of your assignment, and the God that gives you the victory in all things.

> ## Colossians 1:9 (AMPC)
> *9 For this reason, we also, from the day we heard of it, have not ceased to pray and make [[a]special] request for you, [asking] that you may be filled with the [b]full (deep and clear) knowledge of His will in all spiritual wisdom [[c]in comprehensive insight into the ways and purposes of God] and in understanding and discernment of spiritual things— Paul speaks about this confidence he had because of the intimate revelation of the God he served.*
>
> ## 2 Timothy 1:11-12 (TPT)
> *11And he has anointed me as his preacher, his apostle, and his teacher of truth to the nations. 12 The confidence of my calling enables me to overcome every difficulty without shame, for I have an intimate revelation of this God. And my faith in him convinces me that he is more than able to keep all that I've placed in his hands safe and secure until the fullness of his appearance.*

The season of obscurity ensures that you come out knowing the God you serve and not just knowing the church. Obscurity is an invitation to deeper knowledge of God and deeper realms of his glory. It is in this place you come to understand what abiding is. This is why Jesus could say to his disciples that if you have seen me, you have seen the Father because Jesus walked in union with God and remained there because he always valued withdrawing from the crowd to commune and pray to God throughout his entire ministry on earth.

> ### John 15: 4-5 (NLT)
> *4 Remain in me, and I will remain in you. For a branch cannot produce fruit if it is severed from the vine, and you cannot be fruitful unless you remain in me. 5 "Yes, I am the vine; you are the branches. Those who remain in me, and I in them, will produce much fruit. For apart from me, you can do nothing.*

Obscurity trains you on how to abide in Him, and you get to a point where you see God as your vital necessity, which is what he desires from us.

> ### John 29: 13 (AMPC)
> *13 Then you will seek Me, inquire for, and require Me [as a vital necessity] and find Me when you search for Me with all your heart. [Deut. 4:29-30.]*

When you set yourself to intentionally seek God, you can remain encouraged because he promised that when we seek him and require him as a vital necessity to our life, we will find him. This should bring us joy because knowing God should always be our aim. The beautiful thing about knowing God is we get to learn more about ourselves and experience the wonderful process of becoming the very one we behold.

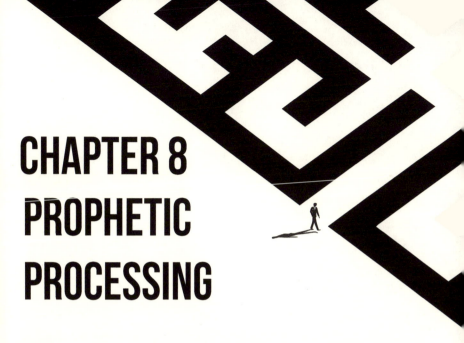

CHAPTER 8
PROPHETIC PROCESSING

Every man or woman God called had clarity in their assignment because they had an encounter, visitation, dream, or instructions from God. After clarity came life experiences that were formed and fashioned for them to go through in order to develop what God proclaimed concerning them. This is God's way of processing and preparing his people. There are moments of learning, and then there are moments of training that can lead to promotion and exaltation. Even Jesus understood the power of being hidden and the importance of only being revealed at his appointed time.

THE LIFE OF JESUS:

Jesus knew his true identity had to be hidden until the proper time, and he concealed the revelation of who he was from men because he had to be crucified; the bible says if they knew his true identity, they wouldn't have done it. Jesus knew enduring the cross would fulfill the plan of God to reconcile humanity back to him, which is what the religious leaders and scribes were trying to keep the people from doing. Jesus had influence, and that frustrated them because they no longer had control over the people. In order to influence, you need power, you need the backing of God, and power is endowed by God; it is given, but it is not automatic because you need wisdom and skill to operate at that level. Power comes from walking in union with God consistently, which allows you to live, move, and breathe as your divine self.

> *Acts 17:28 (NLT)*
> *28 For in him we live, and move, and have our being; as certain also of your own poets have said, For we are also his offspring.*

Jesus would consistently state, "the time has not come for me to be revealed." While reading this scripture, I remember questioning God," Why does every time Jesus does a miracle he tells people not to tell anyone? Why was Jesus doing ministry but wanted who he was to remain hidden? Why did he intentionally hide and humble himself?"The Lord revealed to me that it simply wasn't time for his true identity to be revealed because he knew that his calling brought on the warfare, people would kill him for saying who he was, and it wasn't time for him to be crucified. This also taught me that there are ministry functions, and then there are ultimate assignments and destiny. Jesus had a full-time ministry walking the earth, but his ultimate assignment was being crucified and resurrected so he could ascend and multiply himself on the earth by giving us his

Holy Spirit and allowing us to show up as Him on the earth. Jesus had an assignment to restore man back to God by becoming flesh to experience life as a human. The life he lived on earth shows us how we should live surrendered unto God for the assignment at hand.

Jesus knew who he was, but when his divinity came forth, he wasn't trying to show it off to prove it to anyone because he already knew it himself. Jesus knew that who he was wasn't a performance; it didn't call for that because he was just operating as his divine authentic self, which spoke for itself. This should help us understand that when we understand who we are fully, we can become secure in our identity and calling and gifting, and we will not feel the need to show it off or prove it to anyone because we know it for ourselves. Our confidence will not depend on the response or applause of man, but it will be based on the revelation that comes from God.

John 6: 14-15 (NLT)
14 When the people saw him do this miraculous sign, they exclaimed, "Surely, he is the Prophet we have been expecting!" 15 When Jesus saw that they were ready to force him to be their king, he slipped away into the hills by himself.

Luke 4:36 (NLT)
36 Amazed, the people exclaimed, "What authority and power this man's words possess! Even evil spirits obey him, and they flee at his command!

Jesus was always led by the spirit of God, knew who he was, knew his assignment, and had a revelation of the word to confront Satan and temptation. When people searched for Jesus; he was found in an isolated place praying to God. Jesus never forsake the isolated place with God. Jesus knew this was where the power came from. Private deposits of prayer produced public exploits of power. The world and culture paints this picture of chasing your dreams and manifesting your life, but in the kingdom, the pattern is submission and obedience to God to fulfill His plan for your life.

> *"Private deposits of prayer produced public exploits of power."*

> ### John 7: 1-9 (NLT)
>
> *1 After this, Jesus went around in Galilee. He did not want to go about in Judea because the Jewish leaders there were looking for a way to kill him. 2 But when the Jewish Festival of Tabernacles was near, 3 Jesus' brothers said to him, "Leave Galilee and go to Judea, so that your disciples there may see the works you do. 4 No one who wants to become a public figure acts in secret. Since you are doing these things, show yourself to the world." 5 For even his own brothers did not believe in him.6 Therefore, Jesus told them, "My time is not yet here; for you anytime will do. 7 The world cannot hate you, but it hates me because I testify that its works are evil. 8 You go to the festival. I am not going up to this festival, because my time has not yet fully come." 9 After he had said this, he stayed in Galilee.*

By this time, Jesus had already performed three major miracles; turning water into wine, healing the governmental official son in Capernaum by sending his word to heal, and healing a lame man. Jesus' teachings and miracles revealed that he was sent by God, and caused people to believe in God. Jesus knew he did not come to be glorified but to serve humanity. When he saw the people try to glorify him because of his miraculous signs, he hid. Because it was not about him but about them seeing His father through him.

Jesus' brothers even urged him to go and show off his miracles, show off what you could do so you could become famous; you can't become famous hiding out. This is the trick and the bait the enemy presents to ensnare a people to desire fame in the world instead of valuing the relationship with God and honoring his way of developing and exalting his people. This walk isn't about applause but about assignment completion. Jesus knew it was not his time; Jesus knew it wasn't just about his gift but about who he was. The world hated and was plotting to kill him because of who he carried. Jesus had an assignment; he was secure in who he was so he didn't feel forced to try to show it off. This sense of maturity is developed in obscurity.

Your motive to be used by God shouldn't be for fame and public applause; your priority should be in your secret devotion to God. God publicly rewards those who sow in private. God establishes you; you don't have to establish yourself. You can not have selfish motives and intentions when being used by God because he will not be your leader; applause, praise, and acceptance will be. Jesus knew that it just wasn't about what he could do; it was who he was that people hated and wanted to end, but he had to stay hidden until the time came for him to lay his life down to be the ultimate sacrifice. He had to stay hidden with God. He could do miracles because he abided with God, and knew when to withdraw because his motive wasn't to be seen but to just do his father's will. Jesus knew what he could do, but he also knew the weight and value of who he was. He knew he had to hide because with the unveiling of who he really was and what he really carried comes with warfare; it comes with hate and death.

Jesus knew him being revealed wasn't for popularity or to be seen; it wasn't for his gain naturally; he was just trying to remain hidden until it was time to reveal himself as the Messiah, the son of God. The religious people would think it was blasphemy and crucify him, which was the only way a sinless man could take our place of death for our sins so we can live life reconciled back unto him eternally; we have power here on earth through the blood of Jesus.

Jesus was led by God, not by the people's need of him. Jesus prioritized prayer in isolation and going where his father had said to go with intention. Jesus came with the word and demonstration. There was power and authority in his ministry, which drew a lot of people to him. Jesus was seen and recognized by what he could do, but the revelation of who he was was still hidden. This lets me know that who Jesus is is more important than what he could do.

Your gifting and the things you can do because of God in you aren't what brings the warfare, your identity, who you are, and showing up as that (your divinity), the offspring of the Godhead, is the real threat to hell. This is why we must become skillful in understanding and have a revelation in who we are and our authority because that is the only place we can confront the gates of hell. You con-

PROPHETIC PROCESSING

front lower powers with power from God, and this power has to be entrusted to you. God wants to give us power and dominion; he gives us certain responsibilities and jurisdiction. This is why you have to go to him to figure out where so you can reign there.

When struggling with identity, you look for applause because there is a void in you that doesn't know you, but when you come into Christ, you take on Christ to be him on the earth; your confidence comes from knowing him because his power and glory are inside of you. Your confidence comes from the power of his grace and the miracle of your life that his love has produced. You become confident in who you are and your assignment because you know who is backing you. When you do not know who is backing you, you will try to do things in your own strength, in your carnal and limited view. The only way you can see eternally with no limits is by knowing Him because he will give you his mind and the ability to see dimensionally. Your aim should always be Jesus because knowing who he is reveals and secures your true identity.

"Your aim should always be Jesus because knowing who he is reveals and secures your true identity."

Peter declares his revelation of Jesus in Luke 9:18-21, Jesus warns the disciples not to tell anyone who he was while predicting his death to his disciples to let them know that he would suffer death. Still, he gave them hope in that fact that he would rise again. His ascension would allow him to multiply his seed in the earth by pouring out his spirit upon all flesh, and not just allowing for the Holy

Spirit to be with them but allowing the Holy Spirit to abide and live in them, which is something different than what the disciples experienced when they were walking with him.

Power is produced and made available for you to function and manifest all God has for you in the place of prayer. In obscurity is where you learn how to build a consistent and daily prayer life unto God; it's the place where you learn to build an alter.

> *James 5:16 (AMPC)*
> *16 the earnest (heartfelt, continued) prayer of a righteous man makes tremendous power available [dynamic in its working].*

There came a time when the disciples walking with Jesus tried to operate like him to impact the lives of humanity, but when they tried, it didn't work. When the disciples were alone with Jesus, they asked why they couldn't cast the spirit out.

> *Matthew 17:20-21 (AMPC)*
> *20 He said to them, " Because of the littleness of your faith [that is, your lack of firmly relying on trust]. For truly I say to you, if you have faith [that is living] like a grain of mustard seed, you can say to this mountain, Move from here to yonder place, and it will move; and nothing will be impossible to you. 21 But this kind does not go out except by prayer and fasting.*

This lets us know that we may possess the ability to function, but you need faith, prayer, and fasting (power and authority) to function in it. Power and authority are increased because of your prayer life; it is not automatic.

PROPHETIC PROCESSING

God had already given his disciples power and authority (Matthew 10:1-2) to send them to cast out evil spirits and heal every kind of disease. When the disciples were walking with Jesus and saw him doing the signs that is when they had access to faith. Power and authority came from Jesus' prayer life, which is why they asked Jesus to teach them how to pray (Luke 11:1); they asked for teaching after he gave them power and authority. There was something their efforts to function like Jesus was missing. Power and authority has already been given by God, but prayer and fasting adds weight to it.

> *Luke 20:1-2 (NLT)*
> *1 One day, as Jesus was teaching the people and preaching the Good News in the Temple, the leading priests, the teachers of religious law, and the elders came up to him.*
> *2 They demanded, "By what authority are you doing all these things? Who gave you the right?"*

When the religious scholars challenged Jesus, it was because of his authority. They asked what authority are you coming by ? Basically, they wanted to know who sent him. This is the same question Moses feared answering when God revealed to him his plan for him to deliver the Israelites. Moses needed assurance in who was backing him up so that he could be confident and bold when facing off with the systems of the world. God responded, tell them, I sent you, and proceeded to reveal himself to Moses in private so he could build that faith and fellowship with God to go forth in his assignment. You can't go without the knowledge of the one who sent you, and you can't go feeling insecure or having a lack of trust in the backing of heaven. You can let all fear, insecurity, anxiety, and excuses go once you realize that it's not you, but Christ IN YOU, so you can take the focus off of your shortcomings and yield to him who you can trust to show up strong in your weakness. I think God strategically chooses the places where we are most attacked to use us because he knows we need him to do it.

Acts 19:13-16 (NLT)

13 A group of Jews was traveling from town to town casting out evil spirits. They tried to use the name of the Lord Jesus in their incantation, saying, "I command you in the name of Jesus, whom Paul preaches, to come out!" 14 Seven sons of Sceva, a leading priest, were doing this. 15 But one time, when they tried it, the evil spirit replied, "I know Jesus, and I know Paul, but who are you?" 16 Then the man with the evil spirit leaped on them, overpowered them, and attacked them with such violence that they fled from the house, naked and battered.

When you have no backing, you get overtaken; this is why in order to war at this level, you need backing; you need power and authority, which is produced by daily deposits in the secret place to be endowed with power. Our authority over demonic spirits and systems is our name being written in the lamb's book of life. Jesus made sure that the disciples knew this when they got excited about their authority over demons.

Luke 10:17-20 (AMPC)

17 The seventy returned with joy, saying, Lord, even the demons are subject to us in Your name! 18 And He said to them, I saw Satan falling like a lightning [flash] from heaven. 19 Behold! I have given you authority and power to trample upon serpents and scorpions, and [physical and mental strength and ability] over all the power that the enemy [possesses]; and nothing shall in any way harm you. 20 Nevertheless, do not rejoice at this, that the spirits are subject to you, but rejoice that your names are enrolled in heaven. [Exod. 32:32; Ps. 69:28; Dan. 12:1.]

Power and authority comes when God can put his voice print on yours, and you become one with him and partake in the divine nature to operate as him. Oneness with him comes from abiding. This power is something you already possess but have not been aware of, which is why it wasn't being used. You were unaware and disengaged from this power because you have not come into oneness with him. Oneness with the Father allows you to show up as him and demonstrate his power and glory at any given moment because you live in his presence. This reminds me of the time in my former ministry when I was asked to preach or lead exhortation in a service. I would always find myself rushing to fast and doing all the spiritual disciplines to hear from God and get close to him to produce for him. I didn't realize that being one with God was the place I should live from daily so I wouldn't have to spend time worrying and overworking spiritual duties in order to receive from God.

As a minister and teacher of God's word and also a minister of movement, it is my duty to live a daily life of devotion and worship before God, and when asked to minister before people, they should be receiving from an overflowing well of living water because I abide with God daily privately to live life and not for ministry purposes only. This is such an important concept to grasp because I remember hearing people complain about " being used by God for everybody else but themselves and their personal life. circumstances" I always found something off with this statement because it shows that you could have a public ministry, but you lack private devotion unto God, which becomes unhealthy because you are pouring from an empty cup. Many times in church I would hear people repeat their sad story of being used by God, but feeling like their gift was only benefiting and working for others and not themselves. I believe this was because they lacked fellowship and the right relationship with God to understand their identity and authority. Many get tripped up with what comes with who we are because we have not sat down to learn how to live victoriously.

Going through the season of obscurity helped me find value in knowing God for myself before trying to do this publicly because God doesn't just want to use us, but he cares about our soul wellbeing, and he desires a relationship with us because he designed us to be one with him. If you find yourself in a place of pain because you feel used by God but not known or seen by him, you need to re-evaluate if you know the God you preach, pray, propshey about, and for. There is a possibility to do things for him but never be known by him. This is why obscurity is important because it helps focus your gaze on what and who truly matters so when the time comes for you to be established and exalted and honored in the presence of man, you won't forget the

"His presence produces potency for productivity."

PROPHETIC PROCESSING

importance of having an altar burning before God always. You have to not be focused on productivity, but you must be presence-driven, because his presence produces potency for productivity.

> *Romans 2:29 (NLT)*
> *29 No, a true Jew is one whose heart is right with God. And true circumcision is not merely obeying the letter of the law; rather, it is a change of heart produced by the Spirit. And a person with a changed heart seeks praise from God, not from people.*

Being hidden kills all selfish ambition; being hidden helps you to become skillful in your gifting, and being hidden helps you build a foundation with God. As you think about people in the Bible who knew God, their knowledge of God is what kept them in the storm and trial. Could it be that the reason you are fainting is that you don't really know the God you serve? You just know how to be used by him? Your gift shouldn't lead you; his spirit should because there will be moments where being "busy" doing ministry can be used as a distraction when God is leading you another way, but you can not see it because your desire to flaunt your gift and perfect your gift is a much greater priority than your intimacy with Abba.

Let's examine some lives of people in the Bible that navigated obscurity and prophetic processing

JOHN THE BAPTIST:

> *Luke 1:80 (NLT)*
> *80 John grew up and became strong in spirit. And he lived in the wilderness until he began his public ministry to Israel.*

John the Baptist was born to Elizabeth and Zechariah with an intended purpose to prepare the people for the coming of the Lord. He was born into this world with a prophetic word from heaven stating all that he would do and instructions he would have to follow in order to maintain and carry out his calling. The Bible states that until the time came for him to begin his public ministry, he grew up(matured), became strong in spirit (empowered with strength and vigor), and lived in the wilderness. Wilderness here represents a desert, a solitary, lonely, desolate, and uninhabited place. This description doesn't seem like an exciting place, but you have to remember that God can be the water in your wilderness. In order to navigate through this season, you must build a relationship with the holy spirit and mature as a person. In the wilderness, John the Baptist matured, became strong in spirit, was filled with wisdom, and the grace of God was upon him; these were all the things he needed for his public ministry.

APOSTLES:

Before they became Apostles, they started off as Jesus's disciples that responded to the call to follow him. The disciples walked closely with Jesus and witnessed his power and good works of miracles, signs, and wonders. Jesus taught everyone in parables but always gave the disciples private revelation of everything he taught. This was a place of obscurity for the disciples, which granted them another level of access to God, which came with revelation and understanding. In this time of walking with Jesus, it was really their preparation to do greater works than they saw him doing, but one main thing Jesus always corrected the disciples

PROPHETIC PROCESSING

on was their lack of faith and how it hindered them and their ability to function in the power and authority granted unto them.

During this time of obscurity, the disciples were supposed to develop faith, a greater value system for prayer and fasting, and a greater revelation of who Jesus was and how to operate as Christ in us. When Jesus posed the question, " Who do you say I am?" there was only one disciple, Peter, who had this divine revelation that could have only been revealed by God, the Father. The disciples learned and experienced the cost of following Jesus (Luke 9:23 & Luke 14:25). God taught them how to process rejection and the value of their name being registered in heaven, which gave them a greater understanding of their authority over evil spirits. God taught them parables concerning the kingdom of heaven. God taught them to watch out for false and religious teachers, and to teach the truth they had received and experienced through following him. These are all things you should be learning in obscurity, and one main way the twelve disciples Jesus chose learned so much is because they stayed close to him and inquired of him every chance they got. That is the key to navigating obscurity, asking questions, and sitting still for answers. Before Jesus left the earth, he warned the Apostles about his death, but he gave them hope in the Holy Spirit that he would send because they would need him now that Jesus was gone. Instead of having Jesus with them, they had to be filled with him now by

" That is the key to navigating obscurity, asking questions, and sitting still for answers."

receiving his spirit, which required them to stay in the place of obscurity to be empowered for the journey.

> ## Luke 24:49 (NLT)
> 49 *"And now I will send the Holy Spirit, just as my Father promised. But stay here in the city until the Holy Spirit comes and fills you with power from heaven."*

JOSHUA:

> ## Joshua 1: 1-2 (NLT)
> *1 After the death of Moses, the LORD's servant, the LORD spoke to Joshua, son of Nun, Moses' assistant. He said, 2 "Moses my servant is dead. Therefore, the time has come for you to lead these people, the Israelites, across the Jordan River into the land I am giving them.*

Joshua was Moses's assistant that experienced obscurity. Joshua was chosen as a leader of a tribe to spy out the land the Lord had promised unto the Isrealites. He and another leader, Caleb, were the only ones who came back with the right perspective of the land, which allowed them to be the only ones still standing when it was time to proceed and possess the land. Joshua was then chosen to lead the Israelites after Moses' death. Because Joshua was in place and remained attentive to any task that presented itself in the journey, he was in place for his next place of elevation in leadership. Joshua serving Moses was his place of obscurity; Joshua was an active and responsible participant in his preparation process.

DAVID:

> ## 1 Samuel 16: 11-12 (KJV)
> *11 And Samuel said unto Jesse, Are here all thy children? And he said, There remaineth yet the youngest, and, behold,*

> *he keepeth the sheep. And Samuel said unto Jesse, Send and fetch him: for we will not sit down till he comes hither.12 And he sent and brought him in. Now he was ruddy, and withal of a beautiful countenance, and goodly to look to. And the LORD said, Arise, anoint him: for this is he.*

David was hidden in the fields tending to his father's sheep, which was his current assignment at the time. This shows us that obscurity isn't a place where nothing is happening or lack of work, but it is a place where you must be responsible for what God has entrusted you with in the moment so he can increase you in the proper time. David was chosen, called, and sought after by God and was anointed as king, but there was still a process he would have to endure as the current rejected king, Saul, armor bearer. In obscurity, David was anointed to play the harp, which would drive out the evil spirit that tormented Saul; because David solved this problem, Saul found favor in him. David had to endure being threatened by Saul because of jealousy and envy that began to grow in his heart because of the praise David began to receive after defeating Goliath and winning other battles.

> *1 Samuel 17:34-37 (KJV)*
> *34 And David said unto Saul, Thy servant kept his father's sheep, and there came a lion, and a bear, and took a lamb out of the flock: 35 And I went out after him, and smote him, and delivered it out of his mouth: and when he arose against me, I caught him by his beard, and smote him, and slew him. 36 Thy servant slew both the lion and the bear: and this uncircumcised Philistine shall be as one of them,*

seeing he hath defied the armies of the living God. 37 David said moreover, The LORD that delivered me out of the paw of the lion, and out of the paw of the bear, he will deliver me out of the hand of this Philistine. And Saul said unto David, Go, and the LORD be with thee.

When faced with the giant of Goliath, David was able to use what he had learned in obscurity to assure him that the same God who delivered me then came to deliver me now. David was able to discern the spirit of Goliath, and he knew he had power and authority over him because he had God with him fighting on his behalf. David learned skills to conquer in obscurity, and he also learned more about God and what he has access to because of his union with him. David could handle Goliath because he was able to discern the spirit that was coming against God and his people. So, no matter how intimidating Goliath may have looked compared to David's stature, he approached him boldly because David knew he was not fighting alone and that it was more for him than against him. David stood in his union with God and defeated Goalith with discernment, courage, and skill, which are all products of navigating obscurity.

1 Samuel 17: 45-46 (KJV)
45 Then said David to the Philistine, You come to me with a sword, a spear, and a javelin, but I come to you in the name of the Lord of hosts, the God of the ranks of Israel, Whom you have defied. 46 This day the Lord will deliver you into my hand, and I will smite you and cut off your head. And I will give the corpses of the army of the Philistines this day to the birds of the air and the wild beasts of the earth, that all the earth may know that there is a God in Israel.

DANIEL:

Daniel had wisdom, which qualified him for being chosen along with his three friends for training for royal service in Babylon, which was the system that oppressed the city. Daniel and his friends were trained for 3 years in the culture of Babylon, but Daniel and his friends never bowed down to the culture of Babylon; even though they were called to make an impact in the world's systems, they kept their stance and alliance with God.

> *Daniel 1: 17 (NLT)*
> *17 God gave these four young men an unusual aptitude for understanding every aspect of literature and wisdom. And God gave Daniel the special ability to interpret the meanings of visions and dreams.*

God gave these men special abilities that would separate them from other enchanters and magicians of the other kingdom. When put to the test, Daniel and his friends always presented themselves as superior because of their alliance and sensitivity to the King of Kings. Daniel and his friends never bowed even when the pressures of the culture came up against him he never bowed down, and God preserved and delivered them out of a fiery furnace and Daniel out of the Lion's den, which in return caused the kings and priests of Babylon to acknowledge Daniel's God over all others. Daniel and his friends' abilities from God allowed them to advance to high positions in government, which gave them more influence. The years of training, tests, and promotions were all part of Daniels's place of obscurity. In obscurity, Daniel learned how to seek, pray, and fast unto God for revelation, and he came to know him as the revealer of secrets and never took credit for those abilities; he also learned stewardship; there were many dreams Daniel had in the beginning years of his training that he labored in prayer in intercession and took time to research to gain understanding. Daniel also learned the importance of timing and when to release what God revealed to him in private. Daniel stewarded until his proper time of ascension to higher realms of influence. Daniel's prayer life allowed him to experience angelic encounters and visitations and come into greater realms of divine revelation and knowledge.

JOSEPH:

Joseph also underwent a process until his ultimate elevation to king of Egypt because of his ability to interpret Pharaoh's dream. Right before this elevation, he was placed in jail for the wrong reasons, so he landed in a place he didn't deserve, but God still used the place/ cave for development. This was a place of obscurity for Joseph because after helping the king's baker and cupbearer interpret their dreams, he made sure to ask the cupbearer to remember him when he got out. However, it was two years later that the cupbearer remembered Joseph when a need arose for Pharaoh and his inability to interpret his dream.

> *Genesis 40: 14-15 (NLT)*
> *14 But when all goes well with you, remember me and show me kindness; mention me to Pharaoh and get me out of this prison. 15 I was forcibly carried off from the land of the Hebrews, and even here, I have done nothing to deserve being put in a dungeon."*

SAMUEL:

> ### 1 Samuel 3:1 (NLT)
> 1 Meanwhile, the boy Samuel served the Lord by assisting Eli. Now, in those days, messages from the Lord were very rare, and visions were quite uncommon.

Samuel's season of obscurity looked like he was serving and assisting Eli. When God called Samuel, at first, it sounded like the voice of his leader, Eli. From this point, Samuel did not yet know the Lord because he never got a direct message from the Lord before. But because he was in a position assisting Eli, he was the next Prophet the lord was calling to replace Eli. Samuel's first test was to deliver a very hard and convicting word to Eli, and from that point, he continued to grow in the Lord and became known as a confirmed prophet of the Lord.

> ### 1 Samuel 3:19-20 (NLT)
> 19 As Samuel grew up, the Lord was with him, and everything Samuel said proved to be reliable. 20 And all Israel, from Dan in the north to Beersheba in the south, knew that Samuel was confirmed as a prophet of the Lord.

QUEEN ESTHER:

> ### Esther 2:12 (NLT)
> 12 Before each young woman was taken to the king's bed, she was given the prescribed twelve months of beauty treatments—six months with oil of myrrh, followed by six months with special perfumes and ointments.

> ### Esther 4:13-14 (NLT)
> 13 Mordecai sent this reply to Esther: "Don't think for a moment that because you're in the palace, you will escape

when all other Jews are killed. 14 If you keep quiet at a time like this, deliverance and relief for the Jews will arise from some other place, but you and your relatives will die. Who knows if perhaps you were made queen for just such a time as this?"

Before Esther became Queen, she spent a year enhancing her physical appearance. This shows that God allows people to become that which he has said before they actually step into the role in the natural. She then won the favor of King Xerxes and became queen. Queen Esther became Queen at a very pivotal time because during her reign, there was a plan sent out to destroy her people, and she had to make a decision to use her positional influence to arise and plead for mercy, deliverance, and relief for her nation, the Jews. Taking this stance could mean death, but either way, death would come if she kept quiet, or she could take the risk to deliver her people who wouldn't bow or obey the laws of the king. It took great courage, faith, and sacrifice for Esther to arise for her people; not only did Esther have the appearance of a queen, but she also had the character and the wisdom of a queen, one that could lead her people with great strategy. Even though God was not mentioned throughout the whole book of Esther, it doesn't mean he wasn't there; God intervened in this situation by using human beings to accomplish his will.

DEBORAH:

Judges 4:4-5 (NLT)
4 Deborah, the wife of Lappidoth, was a prophet who was judging Israel at that time. 5 She would sit under the Palm of Deborah, between Ramah and Bethel in the hill country

of Ephraim, and the Israelites would go to her for judgment.
Judges 5:7 (NLT)
7 "There were few people left in the villages of Israel, until Deborah arose as a mother for Israel.

Deborah was a righteous leader with governmental authority in Israel, and people came to her for judgment. There came a time when Deborah's leadership skills were needed in order to deliver to the people of Israel. Deborah had a close relationship with God because she led with great confidence and insight and was the first woman to lead Israel into victory over Sisera. Deborah was already in place, but there came a time when she would have to Arise and take the lead by being led by God. In obscurity, Deborah was able to build her relationship and confidence in God and develop an ear to hear his insight and strategy for victory.

There is a common trend of people's divine abilities from God being used to elevate them, but those people always made sure to give the credit back to God and not themselves; this demonstrates humility and the knowing that we are one with Christ; we are just the vessel that carries him around and allows him to manifest through us to be solutionist and answers to a dying and suffering world. Another common trend is that everyone around the chosen vessels that endured obscurity was able to say they were marked by God, carriers of the God of the holy spirit. They were known as set apart ones that served the most high God and were filled, empowered, and functioned by his spirit. People identified the God in them when they showed up in their divine self, demonstrating their divine abilities, be-

NAVIGATING OBSCURITY

cause when your life is backed up by the power and demonstration of God, people can not deny that power. Obscurity is the place where you become one with the power that lives on the inside of you, and you practice to become skillful in the function the holy spirit grants to you. Your mindset in this process should be, "I'm becoming one with Him, to become skillful in Him."

"I'm becoming one with Him, to become skillful in Him."

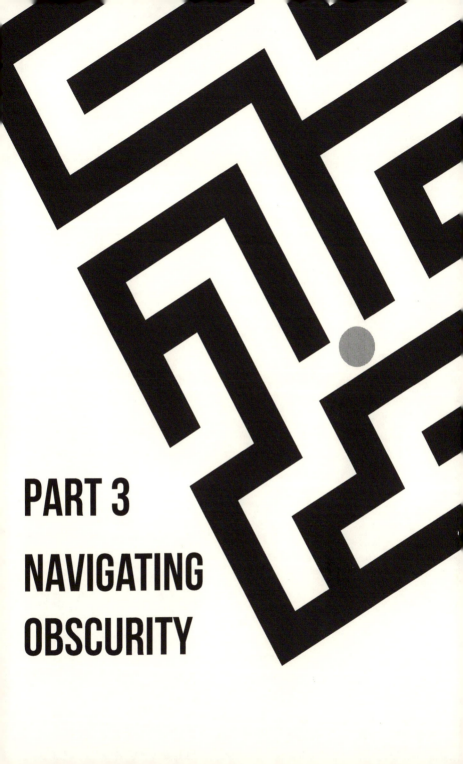

PART 3
NAVIGATING OBSCURITY

CHAPTER 9
ENEMIES OF OBSCURITY

In order to navigate obscurity properly, I would like to share some enemies of obscurity that are sent and empowered by the enemy whose goal is to steal, kill, and destroy everything God desires to build and do through your life. These enemies are barriers that must be confronted and overcome. It is very important to know and be aware of these enemies because God's way is process and development for longevity, while the enemies' plan is designed for you to get where you want to be by any means necessary, even if it requires compromise.

We have to remember that there are no shortcuts in God. These enemies of obscurity must be identified, confronted, and conquered.

> *"These enemies of obscurity must be identified, confronted, and conquered."*

PRIDE

> *1 John 2:16 (NLT)*
> *16 For the world offers only a craving for physical pleasure, a craving for everything we see, and pride in our achievements and possessions. These are not from the Father, but are from this world.*

Pride, by definition, is a feeling of deep pleasure or satisfaction derived from one's own achievements, the achievements of those with whom one is closely associated, or from qualities or possessions that are widely admired. Pride is appearing above others, showing one's self above others, overtopping, conspicuous above others. Having an overweening estimate of one's means or merits, despising others, or even treating them with contempt. Pride lacks honor for others. Pride is not from the father but something that comes from the culture of this world. Pride is first required in our ability to acknowledge our need for God in life. Pride is revealed when you are faced with a situation or experience where you are not the center of attention. Pride resists your ability to be corrected because you think of yourself more highly than others, which Christ tells us not to do so.

Pride is an enemy to navigating obscurity because it is the opposite heart posture and mindset one should have as a follower of Jesus and a kingdom citizen. Pride is an enemy because it taints your view of the importance of the season of being hidden. It is an enemy because being led by pride will lead to you compromising and skipping this season because your pride will not allow you to submit or

ENEMIES OF OBSCURITY

even begin to understand God's intentions behind the way he is choosing to process you. Being led by pride is selfish and is far from how Christ instructs us to live. God desires for us to be meek; we must remember that God will humble the proud but gives grace to the meek. You will know that pride no longer leads you or influences your motives or desired timeline for God to manifest his will when you are okay with submitting to being hidden, isolated, separated, and forced to see the value of the secret place more than the spotlight and applause from man. Pride was and is something that I daily have to put to death because I would see it come up in many spaces of my life when I felt overlooked for opportunities I felt I qualified for. I saw it be confronted when I joined a dance ministry, and being a trained technical dancer was no longer more valuable than carrying the presence and mind of God with every step I took. In obscurity, pride will be revealed, and it is your job to conquer it with the word of God and the desire to please him in humility and allow the process to purge pride out of you.

James 4:6 (AMPC)
6 But He gives us more and more grace (power of the Holy Spirit, to meet this evil tendency and all others fully). That is why He says, God sets Himself against the proud and haughty, but gives grace [continually] to the lowly (those who are humble enough to receive it).

Matthew 5:5 (NLT)
5 God blesses those who are humble, for they will inherit the whole earth.

LUST

> ### 1 John 2:16 (AMPC)
> 16 For all that is in the world—the lust of the flesh [craving for sensual gratification] and, the lust of the eyes [greedy longings of the mind], and the pride of life [assurance in one's own resources or in the stability of earthly things]— these do not come from the Father but are from the world [itself].

These are all the things Jesus was tempted with in the wilderness, but he used the word to answer Satan's temptations and offers. Lust of this world must be confronted in order to ensure there is no place for compromise in you.

COMPARISON & ENVY

Comparing yourself to others may come as a natural instinct, especially when you are being developed for Christ. The only time we should look at others is for mentorship and encouragement, never for measurement because the Bible states that it is unwise.

> ### 2 Corinthians 10:12 (KJV)
> 12 For we dare not number ourselves, or compare ourselves with some who commend themselves. For in measuring themselves by themselves, and comparing themselves among themselves, they are not wise.

Another truth is that comparison robs you of the ability to experience the joy of your own journey because you are always concerned and jealous of others. Comparison is an enemy of navigating obscurity because it takes your focus

ENEMIES OF OBSCURITY

off of what God is doing in you personally. Comparison is a trap of the enemy to force people to become imitators of others because they desire the results of others instead of doing the work to show up as their authentic selves. Comparing yourself to others, where God has them, and how God uses them will never benefit you because you focusing on how you can be like them limits

"Comparing yourself and being envious of others causes you to miss what God wants to reveal to you."

God's ability to show you how he desires to express himself through you. Comparing yourself and being envious of others causes you to miss what God wants to reveal to you. Everyone's journey and calling is different, unique, and personal, so it is unwise to compare yourself with something that doesn't have the same assignment or process as you. We should not compare ourselves to anyone else because our journeys with God are so personal, so you must get to know him for yourself and come to understand his communication and the ways he functions through you; you can not try to copy someone else's methods or formulas because they will not warrant the same results.

Comparison was a trap that I would always fall into because when others had something that I desired or had a certain access to God that I hadn't reached yet, I would get very jealous because it made me feel like I was not part of God, which made me feel rejected and I translated these feelings with the narrative that I believed for a long time that " I am not good enough" when the truth was I just needed to spend time abiding in God to develop my own

NAVIGATING OBSCURITY

anointing and relationship with him, understand my calling from God, and go through the process to get there, not comparing it to anyone else.

REJECTION

Rejection is an enemy to obscurity because without being healed in this place, you will process obscurity as rejection because it is an isolating place to be in because God is calling you to himself. A way rejection sometimes manifests itself in the season of obscurity is when you feel you are being overlooked in certain spaces God has you in. You have to make sure you discern why God has you in specific places because it could be to learn and be poured into instead of you being the one that pours out. Rejection is a place in your soul you must deal with because the season of obscurity will definitely trigger that place and all the emotions that come with it, which will taint the way you view obscurity. I had to realize that the first ever moment where I felt validated, accepted, praised, and affirmed was when I was performing on a stage. The stage became a void filler for me, and my abilities became the things in which I took pride. Rejection must be healed by becoming complete in God because you can not expect to be fed from the same place you need to pour at; the acceptance and applause of man can no longer be the thing that secures you; your foundation must be firm and the only place you can find that is

> *"The acceptance and applause of man can no longer be the thing that secures you; your foundation must be firm and the only place you can find that is knowing your identity in Christ."*

ENEMIES OF OBSCURITY

knowing your identity in Christ.

Rejection for me manifested in my life not because I didn't have people around me, but because I lacked an emotional connection to people, which made me feel unknown, unseen, unloved, and misunderstood because I was left alone to deal with my soul and it was overwhelming because of the trauma I had faced. The healing to rejection is receiving the love of Christ and allowing him to heal that place and be your wonderful counselor and help you process moments of rejection properly because there are times your walk with Christ will seem lonely, and if you are triggered by the feeling of being alone you will have a hard time standing for Christ because you will always compromise to what's comfortable or allows you to fit in because you struggle with standing alone and being secure and not reliving the feelings and emotions rejection once was attached to.

> *Luke 10:16 (NLT)*
> *16 Then he said to the disciples, "Anyone who accepts your message is also accepting me. And anyone who rejects you is rejecting me. And anyone who rejects me is rejecting God, who sent me."*

As Christians you will face rejection, but it should not be taken personally because anyone that rejects you is rejecting the Christ in you. You have to understand that because you have taken on Christ, rejection isn't personal and should not be internalized because you have God on the inside of you. Rejection is unavoidable, but if they reject you, they are rejecting the God in you. Rejection must be healed and processed correctly because if left open, the enemy can use it to tempt you to compromise, not be bold, or avoid confrontation because you fear rejection. You can not show up as God in the earth with a wounded soul. A soul desiring acceptance is a setup for disaster because he already told us that rejection and persecution are the cost of following him. The truth you carry is like a sword; it cuts, it hurts, and it disrupts evil and darkness. Therefore you can't avoid resistance when the message you carry is so holy, set apart, and disruptive. God teaches his disciples on how to respond to rejection.

> *Luke 9:5 (NLT)*
> *5 And if a town refuses to welcome you, shake its dust from your feet as you leave to show that you have abandoned those people to their fate.*

We must learn to shake off rejection and not internalize it or take it personally against our identity. You have been marked and consecrated for God's use, and you will be rejected, but for his namesake, it's not about you but who you carry.

DISTRACTIONS

> *2 Timothy 2: 4 (TPT)*
> *4 For every soldier called to active duty must divorce himself from the distractions of this world so that he may fully satisfy the one who chose him.*

Obscurity is a place that requires focus on God and doing what it takes to please him. The world has a bunch of distractions that will try to influence you to be busy but never productive for God; it will have you doing good things but not God's things. The distractions of this world seem to present great pleasure, but they end in something worthless. The place of obscurity is the place where I begin to count the cost of the anointing and living a life fully surrendered to God. It cost you those distractions that the world may present. Sometimes, a distraction can be something you desire to manifest out of the timing of God. Distractions are an enemy of obscurity because they cause you to live an aimless life, one that doesn't produce anything for God because there is no intention behind what you are doing; it is all led by the desires of your flesh and not the discernment of your spirit.

> *Ephesians 5: 15-17 (TPT)*
> *15-16 So be very careful how you live, not being like those with no understanding, but live honorably with true wisdom, for we are living in evil times. Take full advantage of every day as you spend your life for his purposes. 17 And don't live foolishly, for then you will have discernment to fully understand God's will.*

IGNORANCE

Ignorance is just the absence of revelation and knowledge of the ways of God, which is an enemy to obscurity because without proper understanding or discernment of any season, God allows you to experience, there will be a resistance in your cooperation because you lack understanding and the knowledge of how and why God's ways are what they are. Ignorance also leads to frustration and a cycle of doing the right things at the wrong time, yielding no fruit, which then leads to a lack of faith.

> *Hosea 4: 6 (KJV)*
> *6 My people are destroyed for lack of knowledge: because thou hast rejected knowledge, I will also reject thee, that*

> *thou shalt be no priest to me: seeing thou hast forgotten the law of thy God, I will also forget thy children.*
>
> *James 1: 5-8 (KJV)*
>
> *5 If any of you lack wisdom, let him ask of God, that giveth to all men liberally, and upbraideth not; and it shall be given him. 6 But let him ask in faith, nothing wavering. For he that wavereth is like a wave of the sea driven with the wind and tossed. 7 For let not that man think that he shall receive anything of the Lord. 8 A double minded man is unstable in all his ways.*

IMPATIENCE

Impatience in obscurity sounds like, "does anybody see me? , I should be further than I am; who is going to help me develop in the quickest ways possible?". This kind of thinking is a result of a lack of patience. Patience is a part of the fruit of the spirit of love. Patience is something you must grow in your walk with the Lord because you never know when the season of obscurity will end, and you have to be willing to be patient with the promises of God manifesting in your life. Greatness does take time, and you have to be willing to wait. Impatience is an enemy to obscurity because it will always try to rush the process, never giving you time to be still and sit with God because it doesn't value the journey but only the destination.

This reminds me of Joseph when he was in jail, and he told the people he had ministered to with the interpretation of dreams to remember him when they got out and there was still a season he had to endure. I believe Joseph said, "remember me" because he was tired of this season that did not look like the dream God gave him, but in this

ENEMIES OF OBSCURITY

place of obscurity, Joseph's gifts were being cultivated while also being used for the glory of God and was also a chance for him to grow in his character and understand that God is sovereign and when the time comes the Lord will make it happen. You don't have to rush to this final destination, nor do you have to announce yourself when the problem you are meant to solve presents itself; you will be well equipped to show up in the power of God, and you will have his character because you allowed patience to have its perfect work in you.

> *James 1: 2-4 (KJV)*
> *2 My brethren, count it all joy when ye fall into divers temptations;3 Knowing this, that the trying of your faith worketh patience.4 But let patience have her perfect work, that ye may be perfect and entire, wanting nothing.*

PERFECTIONISM

Obscurity is a place of intense learning, preparation, and training, and a part of learning is being okay with failing, making mistakes, and being open to correction. When you are a perfectionist, your first instinct will be to reject and resist course correction moments and process them in a negative way, which is why perfectionism is an enemy of obscurity. Being that this season is a place of development and train ing, you have to release your will and control to be perfect. The answer to perfectionism is understanding and receiving God's grace.

"The answer to perfectionism is understanding and receiving God's grace."

NAVIGATING OBSCURITY

2 Corinthians 12:9 (NIV)

9 But he said to me, "My grace is sufficient for you, for my power is made perfect in weakness." Therefore, I will boast all the more gladly about my weaknesses, so that Christ's power may rest on me.

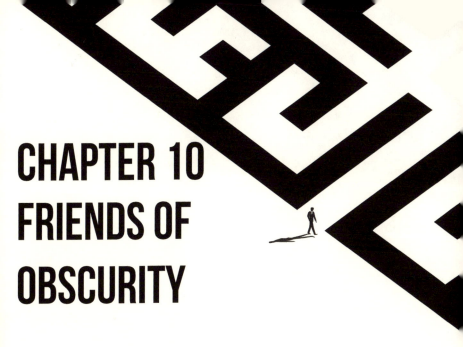

CHAPTER 10
FRIENDS OF OBSCURITY

Now I will highlight some friends of obscurity that will be very beneficial for the journey. These friends come easy when you learn to yield to God in this process.

HUMILITY

God in the flesh humbled Himself and gave up His divine privileges to live among us, accomplish the perfection of life we never could, take upon Himself our punishment, achieve victory over sin, and conquer death. And because of this humility, God gave Him the title of Savior, and in His name, all will bow.

> *Philippians 2:6-9 (NIV)*
> *6 Who, being in very nature God, did not consider equality with God something to be used to his own advantage; 7*

rather, he made himself nothing by taking the very nature of a servant, being made in human likeness. 8 And being found in appearance as a man, he humbled himself by becoming obedient to death— even death on a cross!

9 Therefore God exalted him to the highest place and gave him the name that is above every name.

Humility reflects the heart of the father. There is grace for the humble, humble people can boast about their weaknesses; they don't have an image to upkeep other than the image of God with the mindset that they are what they are because of the grace of God and not their own doings. This is the heart posture of a child of God and one that will be successful in the season of obscurity. Humility is a continual decision to make; humility is something you become by the power of the working of the Holy Spirit in you. Humility is a change of mindset, and heart in your relationship with God and your evaluation of others in relation to yourself. You have to clothe yourself with humility and develop this mindset of a servant. Humility makes you teachable and gives you the ability to honor others above yourself and purges out all selfish ambition.

The mindset one must have while navigating obscurity is one clothed with humility, letting go of pride and desire for fame based on accomplishments and abilities. Your gift and passions should not lead your path or pace; they can only inform you about who you are. You have to trust the way God chooses to develop you. Nothing that has happened in your life is by mistake; it can all work together for the good. You must have the consciousness that your gift is not your worth, but who you are is what pleases God, so I can resist the desire to become fast and know that taking the long way ensures longevity because I have the right relationship with God. I'm not just being used by him, but I have a relationship with him, so I know how to deal with the warfare and battles that come with my calling because God teaches my hands to war in the place of obscurity. Obscurity is the place where you conquer your soul and anything that tries to stand in the way of you becoming and operating as who God says you are.

> *1 Peter 5:6 (NLT)*
> *6 So humble yourselves under the mighty power of God, and at the right time, he will lift you up in honor.*
>
> *Colossians 3: 12-13 (NLT)*
> *12 Since God chose you to be the holy people he loves, you must clothe yourselves with tenderhearted mercy, kindness, humility, gentleness, and patience. 13 Make allowance for each other's faults, and forgive anyone who offends you. Remember, the Lord forgave you, so you must forgive others.*

WHOLENESS

Wholeness is vital in navigating obscurity because you must know that you are complete in Christ and that he is pleased with you because of who you are. Wholeness means you have done the work to allow God to heal your soul so you can process and go through obscurity with his mind instead of the traumas of your soul. God desires for you to be well holistically and in obscurity, there's a place for home to mend all brokenness and heal anything that no longer serves your maturity in him. You can only prosper in life as much as your soul is prospering. You must use this time of obscurity to allow God to produce in you the soul to carry and maintain the calling on your life.

> *Colossians 2: 10 (NLT)*
> *10 So you also are complete through your union with Christ, who is the head over every ruler and authority.*
>
> *3 John 1: 2 (KJV)*
> *2 Beloved, I wish above all things that thou mayest prosper and be in health, even as thy soul prospereth.*

FOCUS & DISCIPLINE

Focusing on what God is saying in this time of obscurity is important because obedience to God is what produces results. In obscurity, the most important thing is knowing Christ and making your devotion and worship to him your highest priority. Also, focus on and in wherever he has placed you to be trained and developed. This can be your church, your school or university, your job, or any place that he sends you to develop the gifts, skills, and callings he has invested in you. These things require focus and intentionality. The revelation of the will of God for your life should organize your life and lead you to make the proper adjustments to house your calling and anointing. Obscurity is the place where you grow in self-discipline because you have accepted and come to an agreement with who and what God says you are, and a disciplined lifestyle leads to a successful life.

ABIDING & STILLNESS

Abiding in Christ is how you get through obscurity and a revelation you must treasure and value throughout your entire walk with the Lord, because apart from Him, you are nothing. Abiding in Christ helps you learn and grow in your ability to hear and be sensitive to his voice, and you fully depend on him for everything he has called you to do and have. In abiding, stillness will become your best friend because you learn how to build your prayer life and your life of worship to God and in that their are moments of stillness you must have to receive from God.

John 15:4 (TPT)

4 So you must remain in life-union with me, for I remain in life-union with you. For as a branch severed from the vine will not bear fruit, so your life will be fruitless unless you live your life intimately joined to mine.

CONSISTENT SEEK

Jeremiah 29:13 (AMPC)

13 Then you will seek Me, inquire for, and require Me [as a vital necessity] and find Me when you search for Me with all your heart. [Deut. 4:29-30.]

Your walk with the Lord has to be sustained by a true hunger and desire to seek him consistently. Requiring God as a vital necessity should be your deepest desire because you understand that you need him daily because you are to live united to him. In order to understand who you are and your specific assignment on the earth, you need consistent seeking. Obscurity is the place where the foundation of joining with Christ begins and must be maintained; you must stay on fire to pursue him daily, always being in a place of pursuit, a place of seeking, and a humble place of simply needing him and him truly being a vital necessity. This consistent seeking first begins with delighting in him, which turns into desire, then a hunger and thirst after Him, and then requiring as a vital necessity.

5 STAGES OF PURSUIT

1. Delight
2. Desire
3. Hunger & Thirst
4. Vital Necessity
5. Wisdom & Revelation

In abiding, you avail yourself to receive wisdom, knowledge, understanding, and access to the mysteries of God that belong to you. Your consistency in abiding and creating an atmosphere for the spirit of the Lord to have his way will open the door for more supernatural activity to take place in your life. In the season of obscurity, not only will you receive revelation of your identity and purpose, but you will also receive wisdom for the current things you may be facing in life that God can use to help someone else.

PATIENT ENDURANCE

Patient endurance is the capacity to hold out or bear up in the face of difficulty, patience, endurance, fortitude, steadfastness, and perseverance. The act or state of patiently waiting for someone or something in expectation. Patient endurance is needed to fulfill God's will, not grow weary in well-doing, and not grow tired or bitter in times of waiting.

Hebrew 10:36 (NLT)

36 Patient endurance is what you need now, so that you will continue to do God's will. Then you will receive all that he has promised.

STEWARDSHIP

In obscurity, God will reveal so much to you and it is worth stewarding because as he gives you piece by piece of who you are, it will begin to come together and paint a full picture of the masterpiece he created you to be. Stewardship of revelation shows God you are interested in what he has to say, so he will begin to trust you with so much more because you value his word and when he speaks. Obscurity is the place where I learned to steward what God gives me because when the time comes for execution, it will be seamless. I won't have to get ready because I spent time preparing in obscurity. Especially things God has revealed and given you the passion to do. Don't be afraid to write the vision because the time will come when you will be glad you stewarded what he gave you. This book is a product of stewarding notes and what seemed like random downloads or small conversations with God of knowledge and wisdom that turned out to be a learning manual for those who would need it.

"I won't have to get ready because I spent time preparing in obscurity."

CHAPTER 11
COPING TO
CONQUERING

I n order to flow in oneness and unity with God, you must subdue and conquer these two areas: the soul and the mind. We are spiritual beings who possess a soul and live in a body. The only thing that looks like Christ after being born again is your spirit. However, your spirit still needs to be trained, fed, and nurtured. Your soul is your job to work out, posses and convert with the help of the word and the Holy Spirit. Your body is your job to upkeep in excellence and holiness through self-control and discipline. Our bodies are the temple of the Holy Spirit, and they are the bodies that house the divine power of God.

A prospering soul and the mind of Christ are what you need in order to navigate obscurity successfully. You can value obscurity when you realize that it is the time of development when you become the person who carries the calling that enhances Christ's expression through you.

NAVIGATING OBSCURITY

It will flow naturally without force or desire to fit any mold or limitations others or yourself may have set for you. You develop your own anointing and your own call with God. After discovery comes the development of that in you, which comes by organizing your life around the understanding of who you are in God.

Obscurity is the place where you no longer stay at potential, but you come into agreement with who you are. The only way you can come into agreement is first letting go of who you used to be, receiving what God says, and doing the work to become that destiny; your calling needs a soul and the mental fortitude that can handle all that comes with it. To whom much is given, much is required. If you go prematurely, you will not be able to handle all that comes with it, which will end in the nonfulfillment of God's plan for your life.

MENTAL MODELS IN OBSCURITY

- I am being built to last, not just for a moment.
- There is a daily lifestyle I must develop and a soul I must have to house my calling.
- I don't get to choose my course, pace, or mentor. Just because they possess something I identify with doesn't mean they are my mentor or valued voice in my life.
- My self worth is not in what I can do, but it is instilled in who I am.
- If I don't know who I am, I can not stand in the day of adversity; no strong roots will quickly be uprooted.
- The only way to know who I am is knowing him. There is value in knowing him.
- I can not fear failure as I learn and develop into who

God has called me to be

- There is a divine time for me to come forth; until then, I will abide, develop, and become skillful.
- I am not led by my gift; I am led by his spirit.

CHAPTER 12
RESPONDING TO
GOD'S INVITATION

How do you respond when God calls your name, not just to receive salvation but choosing to follow and become intimately one with Him? Will you retreat? Will you be too busy? Or will you make time for him to unfold and unveil himself to you in a greater measure? Every calling from God requires a response that turns into a never-ending conversation through abiding in Him daily and choosing to pick up your cross and follow him wholeheartedly. Rather, it is the calling into who you are or God inviting you to new and deeper places in him it all deserves a response and your willing engagement ready to embrace the journey.

Will you respond like this:
NOAH: "So Noah did everything exactly as God commanded him" (Genesis 6:22)

NAVIGATING OBSCURITY

ISAIAH: "Here I am, Send Me" (Isaiah 6:8)

ESTHER: " If I perish, I perish" (Esther 4:16)

MARY: "Be it unto me according to thy word." (Luke 1: 38)

JESUS: "Nevertheless not My will, but Yours, be done" (Luke 22:42)

PAUL: "That I may gain Christ and be found in Him" (Philippians 3:8-9)

APOSTLES: "Left everything and followed him" (Luke 5:11)

SAMUEL: "Speak Lord your servant is listening" (1 Samuel 3:10)

Or will you respond like this:

ABRAHAM: " Laughed to himself in disbelief, how could I become a father at the age of 100?" (Genesis 17:17)

MOSES: "Lord, please send anyone else" (Exodus 4:13)

JEREMIAH: "I can't speak for you! I am too young" (Jeremiah 1:6)

JONAH " Jonah got up and went in the opposite direction to get away from the Lord" (Jonah 1:3)

ZECHARIAH: " How can I be sure this will happen? I'm an old man now. " (Luke 1:18)

God's call needs your agreement not just for the manifestation of his promise over your life but a willing yes to the process. Your devotion to him must come before anything that this life has to offer you. What will your response be to God's call, and what will your posture be in the process of becoming?

> *"God's call needs your agreement not just for the manifestation of his promise over your life but a willing yes to the process."*

RESPONDING TO GOD'S INVITATION

Those are two questions you must decide on to ultimately fulfill the purposes of God. My desire is to live a life poured out to Jesus and to leave this world empty because everything he called me to do was completed, and no time was wasted, and every step I took in the process was intentional. The most valuable thing you will ever gain in fulfilling your purpose is coming into the knowledge of Christ; he should always remain your greatest aim and pursuit. When you abide in him, you can function effortlessly because his glory is so potent on everything you do. When you are a tree planted in him, everything your hands touch should prosper.

Psalm 1:3 (TPT)

3 He will be standing firm like a flourishing tree planted by God's design, deeply rooted by the brooks of bliss, bearing fruit in every season of life. He is never dry, never fainting, ever blessed, ever prosperous.

The key to navigating obscurity is understanding that in order to have and be what God has called you to be, you must surrender to the process of becoming. The formula for success is His Will + His Way + Your Faith = His Fulfilled Plan. This season of obscurity is necessary because before a seed can produce a harvest, it must fall into the ground and die.

John 12:24 (AMPC)

24 I assure you, most solemnly, I tell you, Unless a grain of wheat falls into the earth and dies, it remains [just one grain; it never becomes more but lives] by itself alone. But if it dies, it produces many others and yields a rich harvest.

During the season that the seed is in the ground, and its roots and foundations are being developed and grown into a plant that can not be moved but also produces mush harvest. God will work something in you internally before he will allow it to manifest externally, so you must keep your eyes set on him in all seasons because what obscurity teaches you is the most valuable thing in life is knowing and having intimacy with him. I pray that you can find the beauty, purpose, and power of being hidden so you won't succumb to the temptation to skip this vital part of prophetic processing. When navigating obscurity, you must resist the desire for public praise in exchange for private development. Your time will come, and the Lord will establish you and make you one as bright lights that can not be hidden, and as you trust his process, he will allow everything he has said about you to come to pass.

Philippians 2: 13-15 (KJV)

13 For it is God which worketh in you both to will and to do of his good pleasure. 14Do all things without murmurings and disputings: 15that ye may be blameless and harmless, the sons of God, without rebuke, in the midst of a crooked and perverse nation, among whom ye shine as lights in the world;.

Made in the USA
Columbia, SC
20 March 2025